READ WELL

The Chicken and the Egg

Teacher's Guide

Read Well 1 · Unit 37

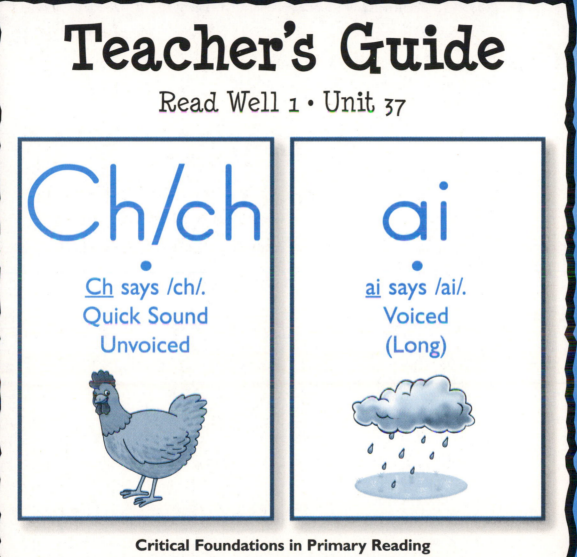

Ch/ch

Ch says /ch/.
Quick Sound
Unvoiced

ai

ai says /ai/.
Voiced
(Long)

Critical Foundations in Primary Reading

Marilyn Sprick, Lisa Howard, Ann Fidanque, Shelley V. Jones

ISBN 13-digit: 978-1-59318-460-5   ISBN 10-digit: 1-59318-460-3   132097/2-12

10 11 12 13 RRDHRBVA 15 14 13 12

SOPRIS WEST EDUCATIONAL SERVICES
A CAMBIUM LEARNING COMPANY

BOSTON, MA • LONGMONT, CO

Table of Contents
Unit 37
The Chicken and the Egg

I I **Voiced** (Word) **Unit A**	Mm /mmm/ **Monkey** Continuous Voiced **Unit B**	Ss /sss/ **Snake** Continuous Unvoiced **Unit 1**	Ee /eee/ **Emu** Continuous Voiced (Long) **Unit 2**	ee /eeee/ **Bee** Continuous Voiced (Long) **Unit 2**	Mm /mmm/ **Monkey** Continuous Voiced **Unit 3**
Aa /aaa/ **Ant** Continuous Voiced (Short) **Unit 4**	Dd /d/ **Dinosaur** Quick Voiced (not duh) **Unit 5**	th /ththth/ **the** Continuous Voiced **Unit 6**	Nn /nnn/ **Nest** Continuous Voiced **Unit 7**	Tt /t/ **Turkey** Quick Unvoiced (not tuh) **Unit 8**	Ww /www/ **Wind** Continuous Voiced (woo) **Unit 9**
Ii /iii/ **Insects** Continuous Voiced (Short) **Unit 10**	Th /Ththth/ **The** Continuous Voiced **Unit 10**	Hh /h/ **Hippo** Quick Unvoiced (not huh) **Unit 11**	Cc /c/ **Cat** Quick Unvoiced (not cuh) **Unit 12**	Rr /rrr/ **Rabbit** Continuous Voiced **Unit 13**	ea /eaeaea/ **Eagle** Continuous Voiced (Long) **Unit 13**
Sh/sh /shshsh/ **Sheep** Continuous Unvoiced **Unit 14**	Kk, -ck /k/ **Kangaroo** Quick Unvoiced (not kuh) **Unit 15**	oo /oooo/ **Moon** Continuous Voiced (Long) **Unit 16**	ar /ar/ **Shark** Voiced (R-Controlled) **Unit 17**	Wh/wh /wh/ **Whale** Quick Voiced **Unit 18**	Ee /ĕĕĕ/ **Engine or Ed** Continuous Voiced (Short) **Unit 19**
-y /-yyy/ **Fly** Continuous Voiced (Long) **Unit 20**	Ll /lll/ **Letter** Continuous Voiced **Unit 21**	Oo /ooo/ **Otter** Continuous Voiced (Short) **Unit 22**	Bb /b/ **Bat** Quick Voiced (not buh) **Unit 23**	all /all/ **Ball** Voiced **Unit 23**	Gg /g/ **Gorilla** Quick Voiced (not guh) **Unit 24**
Ff /fff/ **Frog** Continuous Unvoiced **Unit 25**	Uu /uuu/ **Umbrella** Continuous Voiced (Short) **Unit 26**	er /er/ **Sister** Voiced (R-Controlled) **Unit 27**	oo /oo/ **Book** Voiced (Short) **Unit 27**	Yy /y-/ **Yarn** Quick Voiced **Unit 28**	Aa /a/ **Ago** Voiced (Schwa) **Unit 28**
Pp /p/ **Pig** Quick Unvoiced (not puh) **Unit 29**	ay /ay/ **Hay** Voiced **Unit 29**	Vv /vvv/ **Volcano** Continuous Voiced **Unit 30**	Qu/qu /qu/ **Quake** Quick Unvoiced **Unit 31**	Jj /j/ **Jaguar** Quick Voiced (not juh) **Unit 32**	Xx /ksss/ **Fox** Continuous Unvoiced **Unit 33**
or /or/ **Horn** Voiced (R-Controlled) **Unit 33**	Zz /zzz/ **Zebra** Continuous Voiced **Unit 34**	a_e /a_e/ **Cake** Bossy E Voiced (Long) **Unit 34**	-y /-y/ **Baby** Voiced **Unit 35**	i_e /i_e/ **Kite** Bossy E Voiced (Long) **Unit 35**	ou /ou/ **Cloud** Voiced **Unit 36**
ow /ow/ **Cow** Voiced **Unit 36**	Ch/ch /ch/ **Chicken** Quick Unvoiced **Unit 37**	ai /ai/ **Rain** Voiced (Long) **Unit 37**	igh /igh/ **Flight** Voiced (Long) **Unit 38**	o_e /o_e/ **Bone** Bossy E Voiced (Long) **Unit 38**	ir /ir/ **Bird** Voiced (R-Controlled) **Unit 38**

Introduction
The Chicken and the Egg

Story Notes

We have a long history of teaching life's lessons via stories about animals—old favorites like Aesop's Fables, the "Three Little Pigs," and the "Little Red Hen." Children begin Unit 37 with a story about a vain and snooty hen named Chuckella.

Chuckella's story is followed by an expository passage about the development of a chick. Children learn interesting facts and then create their own graphic organizer of the chick's development from egg to hen or rooster.

Recommended Read Aloud

For reading outside of small group instruction

Egg to Chick by Millicent E. Selsam

Nonfiction • Expository

This Reading Rainbow® selection carefully traces the development of a chicken—from egg and sperm through its twenty-one days in an egg. Children will be fascinated with drawings and pictures of a developing chick at three, five, seven, ten, thirteen, sixteen, and nineteen days.

Read Well Connection

The expository passage in *Read Well* provides solid background knowledge for the more detailed look at the development of a chicken in Selsam's book. This Level 3 "I Can Read Book®" is almost decodable for students completing *Read Well* Unit 37.

NOTE FROM THE AUTHORS

You and your children have worked hard. We hope you've had fun. Though your students are near the end of *Read Well 1*, don't rush. Continue to adhere to the principles of mastery-based instruction. Skills learned will be maintained.

New and Important Objectives
A Research-Based Reading Program
Just Right for Young Children

Oral Language
Phonemic Awareness
Phonics
Fluency
Vocabulary
Comprehension

◆◆ **Oral Language**

In Units 21–38, language patterns are provided for high-frequency words and for some of the low-frequency words that are likely to require clarification.

Phonemic Awareness

Isolating Beginning, Middle, Ending Sounds, Segmenting, Blending, Rhyming, Onset and Rime

Phonics

Letter Sounds and Combinations

★ch, ★Ch, ★ai

Review • Ss, Ee, ee, Mm, Aa, Dd, th, Nn, Tt, Ww, Ii, Th, Hh, Cc, Rr, ea, sh, Sh, Kk, -ck, oo, ar, wh, Wh, e (short), -y (as in "fly"), Ll, Oo, Bb, all, Gg, Ff, Uu, er, oo (as in "book"), Yy, a (schwa), Pp, ay, Vv, Qq, Jj, Xx, or, Zz, a_e, -y (as in "baby"), i_e, ou, ow

Pattern Words

★addition, ★barnyard, ★Barnyard, ★<u>beaks</u>, ★begin, ★beginning, ★beginnings, ★begins, ★<u>between</u>, ★bit, ★bleach, ★bragging, ★brain, ★bunch, ★buzzing, ★cackled, ★chain, ★chap, ★chatterbox, ★cheep, ★chick, ★chicken, ★chickens, ★Chicken's, ★chicks, ★chimpanzee, ★chip, ★chop, ★Chuckella, ★Chuckella's, ★<u>chuckle</u>, ★chump, ★cluck, ★Cluck, ★clucked, ★each, ★Each, ★fluff, ★fluffs, ★form, ★forming, ★fossil, ★fraction, ★<u>gather</u>, ★<u>gotten</u>, ★hatch, ★Hatches, ★hatching, ★impressed, ★indeed, ★inside, ★laying, ★lays, ★life, ★Life, ★mate, ★Mike, ★morning, ★named, ★peeked, ★peeking, ★preach, ★prizes, ★reach, ★ribbit, ★Ribbit, ★robin, ★<u>rooster</u>, ★<u>Rooster</u>, ★<u>roosters</u>, ★safe, ★scratchy, ★She's, ★side, ★slide, ★snake, ★sneered, ★snooty, ★snout, ★specks, ★speech, ★speechless, ★such, ★switch, ★switching, ★Switching, ★teach, ★time, ★times, ★train, ★vain, ★Vain, ★which, ★while, ★white, ★wide, ★wife, ★wise, ★witty, ★Zeb

Review • *about, act, After, all, All, am, an, and, around, asked, at, At, ate, back, be, began, big, bigger, black, bring, brown, Brown, Brown's, but, by, called, came, can, cats, cloudy, cold, crack, day, days, dear, did, Did, didn't, different, dog, dripping, eat, Every, expect, Fact, facts, Farmer, *fiction, fifteen, fine, food, for, forgot, found, get, gets, getting, going, got, green, had, happens, happy, hard, he, hear, helps, hen,

◆◆ = Oral language patterns   ★ = New in this unit   Underline = New words introduced in context

Pattern Words *(continued)*

Hen, hens, her, hid, house, how, How, however, in, In, it, It, It's, just, Just, keep, lack, lake, last, lay, leaves, left, let, Let's, lick, like, long, looked, market, me, must, my, My, need, Needs, nest, next, no, not, Not, now, Now, off, on, out, Out, part, peck, picked, quick, *rain, red, rest, run, same, say, see, seem, sell, set, seven, she, She, shell, short, shout, sing, sit, sits, sitting, small, so, So, Soon, start, started, still, sweet, take, tame, team, tell, that, That, them, then, Then, this, This, thousands, three, Tim, Tom, too, tooth, town, twenty, until, Until, up, upon, upset, way, we, We, went, wet, when, When, will, win, wings, yuck

*Note: Occasionally a Tricky Word will be gradually moved from the Tricky Word category to the Pattern Word category as a pattern is established.

Tricky Words

⭐*crocodile,* ⭐*develop,* ⭐*developing,* ⭐*dinosaur,* ⭐*Dinosaur,* ⭐*does,* ⭐*fathers,* ⭐*head,* ⭐*heads,* ⭐*lesson,* ⭐*Lesson,* ⭐*mothers,* ⭐*Once,* ⭐*pretty,* ⭐*Pretty,* ⭐*themselves*

Review • a, A, again, another, any, are, as, because, become, Before, come, couldn't, do, done, don't, egg, Eggs, even, Even, everyone, from, gone, goose, have, I, I'm, into, Into, is, isn't, laugh, laughed, legs, listen, little, many, more, mother, of, one, other, said, should, the, The, their, Their, there, There, There's, they, They, to, To, together, two, very, want, was, water, were, what, What, Where, Who, would, wouldn't, you, your

Comprehension

Comprehension Strategies

Building Knowledge, Priming Background Knowledge, Making Connections, Predicting, Identifying, Describing, Defining, Applying, Explaining, Inferring, Verifying, Classifying, Summarizing, Evaluating, Monitoring Comprehension, Locating Information, Sequencing

Story Elements

Title, Who (Main Character), Where (Setting), Want (Goal), Problem, What (Action), Conclusion

Story Vocabulary

⭐Hen, ⭐Rooster, ⭐Vain, ⭐Lesson, ⭐Snooty, Fact, Fiction

Text Structure

Beginning, Middle, End

Expository Elements

Fact, Topic

Genre

Fiction • Narrative

Nonfiction • Expository

Lessons

⭐Characters who are snooty and vain are also often foolish.

⭐Tricking someone either teaches the wrong lesson or doesn't teach a lesson at all.

⭐From egg to chick to hen or rooster, a chicken's cycle of life is predictable, yet wondrous.

Written Response

Sentence Illustration, Sentence Completion, List, Sentence Comprehension—Multiple Choice, Summarizing—Story Map, ⭐Composing—End, Conventions— Beginning Capital, Period

Fluency

Accuracy, Expression, Phrasing, Rate

Daily Lesson Planning

PACING

Some students will begin the process of learning to read slowly but make rapid progress later. If students complete Unit 38 by the end of the year, they will be at or above a beginning second grade reading level. Groups that are working at a slower pace may require more intensive *Read Well* instruction and practice. (See *Getting Started: A Guide to Implementation*.)

ASSESSMENT

Upon completion of this unit, assess each student and proceed to Unit 38 as appropriate.

SAMPLE LESSON PLANS

The sample lesson plans illustrate how materials can be used for students with different learning needs. Each lesson plan is designed to provide daily decoding practice and story reading.

WEAK PASS CAUTION

If a student or students receive a Weak Pass on the previous two units, do not simply continue forward. See "Making Decisions" for Intervention Options.

3-DAY PLAN		
Day 1 • Decoding Practice 1 • Stories 1 and 2 • Comprehension Work 1b* • Comprehension Work 2* • Homework 1, Stories 1 and 2*	**Day 2** • Decoding Practice 2 • Stories 3 and 4 • Comprehension Work 3a* • Comprehension Work 4* • Homework 2, Story 4*	**Day 3** • Decoding Practice 3 • Stories 5 and 6 and Summary • Comprehension Work 5* • Comprehension Work 6a* • Homework 3, Story 5* • Homework 4, Story 6*

Note: To avoid excessive seatwork, 3- and 4-Day Plans omit or adjust use of Skill Work. If appropriate, Skill Work 1a and 3b can be used anytime during or after this unit as independent work or homework.

4-DAY PLAN			
Day 1 • Decoding Practice 1 • Stories 1 and 2 • Comprehension Work 1b* • Comprehension Work 2* • Homework 1, Stories 1 and 2*	**Day 2** • Decoding Practice 2 • Stories 3 and 4 • Comprehension Work 3a* • Comprehension Work 4* • Homework 2, Story 4*	**Day 3** • Decoding Practice 3 • Story 5 • Comprehension Work 5* • Homework 3, Story 5*	**Day 4** • Decoding Practice 4 • Story 6 and Summary • Comprehension Work 6a* • Comprehension Work 6b* • Homework 4, Story 6*

---

* From *Read Well* Comprehension and Skill Work (workbook), *Read Well* Homework (blackline masters), or Extra Practice in this book.

6-DAY PLAN

Day 1	Day 2	Day 3
• Decoding Practice 1 • Story 1 • Skill Work 1a* (Optional) • Comprehension Work 1b*	• Review Decoding Practice 1 • Story 2 • Comprehension Work 2* • Homework 1, Stories 1 and 2*	• Decoding Practice 2 • Story 3 • Comprehension Work 3a* • Skill Work 3b* (Optional)
Day 4	**Day 5**	**Day 6**
• Review Decoding Practice 2 • Story 4 • Comprehension Work 4* • Homework 2, Story 4*	• Decoding Practice 3 • Story 5 • Comprehension Work 5* • Homework 3, Story 5*	• Decoding Practice 4 • Story 6 and Summary • Comprehension Work 6a* • Homework 4, Story 6*

PRE-INTERVENTION AND INTERVENTION
See *Getting Started: A Guide to Implementation* for information on how to achieve mastery at a faster pace with students who require eight or more days of instruction.

8-DAY PLAN • *Pre-Intervention*

Day 1	Day 2	Day 3	Day 4
• Decoding Practice 1 • Story 1 • Skill Work 1a* (Optional) • Comprehension Work 1b*	• Review Decoding Practice 1 • Story 2 • Comprehension Work 2* • Homework 1, Stories 1 and 2*	• Decoding Practice 2 • Story 3 • Comprehension Work 3a* • Skill Work 3b* (Optional)	• Review Decoding Practice 2 • Story 4 • Comprehension Work 4* • Homework 2, Story 4*
Day 5	**Day 6**	**Day 7**	**Day 8**
• Decoding Practice 3 • Story 5 • Comprehension Work 5* • Homework 3, Story 5*	• Decoding Practice 4 • Story 6 and Summary • Comprehension Work 6a* • Homework 4, Story 6*	• Extra Practice 1* • Extra Practice 1 Fluency Passage*	• Extra Practice 2* • Extra Practice 2 Fluency Passages*

10-DAY PLAN • *Intervention*

Day 1	Day 2	Day 3	Day 4	Day 5
• Decoding Practice 1 • Story 1 • Skill Work 1a* (Optional) • Comprehension Work 1b*	• Review Decoding Practice 1 • Story 2 • Comprehension Work 2* • Homework 1, Stories 1 and 2*	• Decoding Practice 2 • Story 3 • Comprehension Work 3a* • Skill Work 3b* (Optional)	• Review Decoding Practice 2 • Story 4 • Comprehension Work 4* • Homework 2, Story 4*	• Decoding Practice 3 • Story 5 • Comprehension Work 5* • Homework 3, Story 5*
Day 6	**Day 7**	**Day 8**	**Day 9**	**Day 10**
• Decoding Practice 4 • Story 6 and Summary • Comprehension Work 6a* • Homework 4, Story 6*	• Extra Practice 1* • Extra Practice 1 Fluency Passage*	• Extra Practice 2* • Extra Practice 2 Fluency Passages*	• Extra Practice 3* • Extra Practice 3 Fluency Passage*	• Extra Practice 4* • Extra Practice 4 Fluency Passage*

Materials and Materials Preparation

Core Lessons

Teacher Materials

READ WELL MATERIALS

- Unit 37 Teacher's Guide
- Sound and Word Cards for Units 1–37
- Game markers (optional for use with cover-up activities)
- *Assessment Manual* or page 56

SCHOOL SUPPLIES

- Stopwatch or watch with a second hand

Student Materials

READ WELL MATERIALS

- Decoding Book 4 for each student
- Unit 37 Storybook for each student
- Unit 37 Comprehension and Skill Work for each student (My Activity Book 4)
- Unit 37 Certificate of Achievement (blackline master page 57)
- Unit 37 Homework for each student (blackline masters)
  See *Getting Started* for suggested homework routines.

SCHOOL SUPPLIES

- Pencils, colors (optional—markers, crayons, or colored pencils)

> Make one copy per student of each blackline master as appropriate for the group.
>
> *Note:* For new or difficult Comprehension and Skill Work activities, make overhead transparencies from the blackline masters. Use the transparencies to demonstrate and guide practice.

Extra Practice Lessons

Note: Use these lessons only if needed.

Student Materials

READ WELL MATERIALS

- Unit 37 Extra Practice 1 and 2 for each student (blackline master pages 59 and 63)
- Unit 37 Extra Practice 1, 2, 3, and 4 Fluency Passages for each student (blackline master pages 60, 64, 66, 68)
- Take-Home Game (blackline master page 61)

SCHOOL SUPPLIES

- Pencils, colors (markers, crayons, or colored pencils)
- White boards or paper

Important Tips

In this section, you will find:

⭐ **Building Oral Reading Fluency**

Skillful readers read with both accuracy and speed—processes that allow a gateway to comprehension of written text. Skillful readers continue to build fluency for many years. Review procedures for improving oral reading fluency. Consider tape-recording to increase motivation and self-monitoring. Young children love to hear themselves and will practice to improve.

⭐ **Increasing Sophistication— Guiding Comprehension**

Narrative Comprehension: In Unit 37, students read about a foolish chicken who is both *snooty* and *vain*. The Teacher's Guide will assist you in helping children identify the actions that define a character.

Expository Comprehension: Next, you will guide students through two levels of understanding as they read an expository passage for facts, and then reread the passage to trace the life cycle of a chicken.

⭐ **Generalizing**

Natural readers can be encouraged to read widely by reading from a variety of books related to *Read Well* topics. Learn procedures for having your group read and share information from other books.

High-Frequency Words

By Units 37 and 38, *Read Well* students are able to decode a large proportion of high-frequency words. For English Language Learners and children with language delays, this decoding ability provides a vehicle for practicing useful language patterns.

A cumulative list of high-frequency words is provided for additional emphasis and practice across settings.

★Building Oral Reading Fluency

PURPOSE

By Unit 37, many students are rapidly building fluency through practice—with little need for additional instructional intervention. Other students require an ongoing focus on fluency to become proficient readers.

DAILY PROCEDURES

Continue following *Read Well's* story-reading procedures to build accuracy and speed. On a daily basis, continue to:

- Have students track words with their fingers during story reading.
- Adhere to the accuracy goal during story reading.
- Gently correct errors during story reading.
- Practice difficult words between readings.
- Work on expressive reading.
- Provide multiple opportunities for repeated practice on the Solo Stories.

ADDITIONAL PRACTICE

Provide additional practice for students who have difficulty or who barely meet the desired fluency on assessments. With these students, work first on accuracy, then expression, and finally on speed with short practice sessions. Five extra minutes with a trained instructional assistant, parent volunteer, or older student can ensure success for many high-risk students. Use Solo Stories, Homework, and Extra Practice Fluency Passages for these sessions.

INDIVIDUAL INTERVENTIONS: ACCURACY AND FLUENCY

Encourage accuracy by having students practice and then tape-record Solo Stories, Homework, and Extra Practice.

- Use the Personal Goal Setting form in *Getting Started: A Guide to Implementation*.
- Have the student practice five to ten minutes each day.

Option 1

- Have students practice a story for the purpose of making a tape recording. Encourage children to sound out difficult words and read expressively. As the student reads, draw a star at the end of each sentence read correctly.
- Tape-record the passage.
- Have the student listen to his or her recording and mark any errors on his or her story.
- Have the student practice difficult words and reread difficult sentences.
- Have the student record the passage a second time. Acknowledge improvements.

Option 2

- Follow basic timing procedures with four repeated readings. Use the charts provided on Extra Practice Fluency Passages.
- Between readings, guide practice on a paragraph. Read with the student, using exaggerated expression and a speed slightly above the student's reading rate. Finally, have the student read the paragraph independently.

★Increasing Sophistication
Guiding Comprehension

NARRATIVE COMPREHENSION

In Unit 37, students learn the vocabulary words "snooty" and "vain." As the concepts are sophisticated, the Teacher's Guide provides added information to help you draw students' attention to the actions that define "snooty" and "vain." With each encounter of the words, students increase their depth of understanding.

EXPOSITORY COMPREHENSION

In Unit 37, students also read an expository passage about the life cycle of a chicken. Unlike previous units, with the first reading, students will read the passage aloud and verbally rehearse important facts. On the second reading, you will set the purpose for silent reading to draw students' attention to the life cycle of the chicken.

Read the Teacher's Guide for assistance as you guide students to greater levels of sophistication.

★ Generalizing

PURPOSE

Natural readers can often generalize their skills with ease to other materials. Encourage students to read widely.

PROCEDURES

1. Have students identify a topic of interest from the themes they have read about in their *Read Well* Storybooks. Bring in books and have students bring in books on those topics. Explain that some of the books were written for much older students or adults.
2. Let each student pick a paragraph from one of the books to read to the group. Encourage them to choose from a variety of books.
3. Have students scan the paragraph and identify any words they do not know how to pronounce.
4. Put the identified words on the board. Have the whole group practice decoding the new words.
5. Give the students a few minutes to practice their passages.
6. Let each student read his or her passage. Students who are listening should be prepared to share two or three interesting facts that they learned.

(If you have additional time, low-performing students would benefit from a continued focus on instruction and practice in *Read Well*—through the completion of *Read Well 1* and *Read Well Plus*.)

High-Frequency Words

PURPOSE

Fry (2000) found that 300 words make up about 65% of all written materials. By Unit 38, students have learned and practiced an impressive 244 of these important words. (The remaining fifty-six words are learned in *Read Well Plus*.) With growing decoding skills, English Language Learners and children with language delays have the added value of being able to practice needed language patterns in both written and oral form.

THE FIRST HUNDRED WORDS

By Unit 38, students learn ninety-six of the first hundred words: *the, of, and, a, to, in, is, you, that, it, he, was, for, on, are, as, with, his, they, I, at, be, this, have, from, or, one, had, by, word, but, not, what, all, were, we, when, your, can, said, there, use, an, each, which, she, do, how, their, if, will, up, other, about, out, many, then, them, so, some, her, would, make, like, him, into, time, has, look, two, more, go, see, no, way, could, people, my, than, first, water, been, call, who, its, now, find, long, down, day, did, get, come, made, may, part*

Words not introduced by Unit 38: *these, write*, number*, oil*

THE SECOND HUNDRED WORDS

By Unit 38, students learn seventy-seven of the second hundred words: *sound, take, only, little, work, year, live, me, back, give, very, after, thing, just, name, good, man, think, say, great, where, help, before, right, too, mean, old, any, same, tell, boy, came, want, also, around, form, three, small, set, put, end, does, another, well, must, big, even, such, because, why, ask, went, men, read, need, land, different, home, us, move, try, hand, again, off, play, air, away, animal, house, letter, mother, found, still, learn, should, America, world*

Words not introduced by Unit 38: *over, new, know, place, most, our*, sentence, through, much*, line*, follow, show, large, turn, here, kind, picture, change, spell*, point, page, answer, study**

THE THIRD HUNDRED WORDS

By Unit 38, students learn seventy-one of the third hundred words: *high, every, near, add, food, between, plant, last, school, father, keep, tree, never, start, earth, light, head, under, story, left, don't, while, along, might, close, something, seem, next, hard, example, begin, always, paper, together, got, often, run, until, side, feet, car, night, walk, white, sea, began, took, river, four, state, once, book, hear, stop, second, later, miss, eat, watch, far, really, let, girl, sometimes, mountain, cut, soon, list, song, leave, it's*

Words not introduced by Unit 38: *own, below, country, city, eye, thought, saw, few, open, life*, those*, both, group, important, children*, mile*, grow, carry, without*, idea, enough, face, Indian, almost, above, young, talk*, being, family**

*These words have not been introduced by Unit 38, but are decodable based on students' skills.

From Fry, E. B., Kress, J. E., & Fountoukidis, D. L. (2000). *The Reading Teacher's Book of Lists*. Jossey-Bass: San Francisco. Reprinted with permission of John Wiley & Sons, Inc.

How to Teach the Lessons

Teach from this section. Each instructional component is outlined in an easy-to-teach format. Special tips are provided to help you nurture student progress.

Decoding Practice 1

- Unit Introduction
- Story 1, Solo
- Skill Work Activity 1a
- Comprehension Work Activity 1b
- Story 2, Solo
- Comprehension Work Activity 2

Decoding Practice 2

- Story 3, Solo
- Comprehension Work Activity 3a
- Skill Work Activity 3b
- Story 4, Solo
- Comprehension Work Activity 4

Decoding Practice 3

- Story 5, Solo
- Comprehension Work Activity 5
- Story 6, Solo
- Fact Summary
- Comprehension Work Activity 6a
- Comprehension Work Activity 6b

Decoding Practice 4

Review Solo Stories

BUILDING INDEPENDENCE
Next Steps • Principles of Instruction

For Units 21–38, follow the scaffolded principles of instruction below.

Provide demonstration and/or guided practice only with:
- New sounds
- Pattern words with new sounds
- New Tricky Words
- New multisyllabic words

Provide independent practice (practice without your assistance or voice) on:
- New and review pattern words with known sounds
- Review Tricky Words
- Review multisyllabic words

If students make errors, provide appropriate corrections.
- Have students identify any difficult sound and then sound out the word. Provide discrimination practice.
- Reintroduce difficult Tricky Words based on the initial introduction procedures.

If students require your assistance on words with known sounds, evaluate placement and consider a Jell-Well Review.

11

❶ SOUND REVIEW

◆◆ **❷ NEW SOUND INTRODUCTION**

★ **New sound: /ch/ as in "chicken"**
Make sure students can hear the difference between /ch/ and /sh/.

> ◆◆ **FOR ENGLISH LANGUAGE LEARNERS AND CHILDREN WITH LANGUAGE DELAYS**
> Throughout Decoding Practice and Extra Practice, provide repeated use of the language patterns—both within and outside of lessons.

◆◆ **❸ ACCURACY AND FLUENCY BUILDING WITH BOSSY E**

- Remind students that the Bossy E jumps over and makes the letter i say its name. For each word, have students say the underlined letter name, then read the word.
- Repeat practice on the column, building accuracy first and then fluency.

❹ ACCURACY AND FLUENCY BUILDING

Repeat practice on each column, building accuracy first and then fluency.

★ **New sound: /ai/ as in "rain"**

- For the Pencil Column, say something like:

  Tell me the word. (rain)

  Tell me the first sound in "rain." (/rrr/)

  Tell me the next sound. /āāā/

  Ai says /āāā/.

  The next two words rhyme with "rain." Read the words. (vain, chain)

- Have students say the underlined part, then read each word.
- Have students read the column.

❺ SOUNDING OUT SMOOTHLY

Provide repeated practice. Mix group and individual turns, independent of your voice.

❻ MULTISYLLABIC WORDS

- Have students silently figure out each word then read it. Use the words in sentences.
- Provide repeated practice. Mix group and individual turns, independent of your voice.

◆◆ **❼ TRICKY WORDS**

★ **New Tricky Words: "Once," "pretty," "head"**

- Introduce the Tricky Word "once." Say something like:

  Your new word "once" is very tricky. It doesn't sound out at all. Many stories begin with "once." "Once upon a time . . ." Read the word three times. (Once, Once, Once)

- For the word "pretty," have students try to figure the word out themselves. Tell students the correct pronunciation, if needed, then have them read the word "pretty" three times.
- Before students read the word "head," tell them that ea sometimes says /ĕĕĕ/. Then have them try to figure out the word "head" for themselves. Tell students the correct pronunciation, if needed, then have them read the word "head" three times.
- Have students read the row. Repeat, mixing group and individual turns.

❽ DAILY STORY READING

Proceed to the Unit 37 Storybook. See Daily Lesson Planning for pacing suggestions.

❾ COMPREHENSION AND SKILL WORK ACTIVITY I AND/OR ACTIVITY 2

See pages 20, 21, and/or 25.

UNIT **37** DECODING PRACTICE I
(For use with Stories I and 2)

MR. Z'S TEAM EXPECTATIONS
Provide a quick review of expectations before starting the lesson.

1. Sit up.

2. Follow directions.

3. Help each other.

4. Work hard and have fun.

I. **SOUND REVIEW** Use Sound Cards for Units 1–36.

★2. **NEW SOUND INTRODUCTION** Introduce /ch/ as in "chicken." For each word, have students say the underlined part, then read the word.

● ★ | ch | chicks   each   hatch   such

▲   teach   chickens   ★ Chuckella

3. **ACCURACY/FLUENCY BUILDING WITH BOSSY E** For each word, have students say the underlined part, then read the word.

☆ time   wife   wise   prizes   while   white

★4. **ACCURACY/FLUENCY BUILDING** For each column, have students say any underlined part, then read each word. Next, have students practice the column.

♥	✎	✈
Brown	★rain	snooty
found	vain	witty
around	chain	very
house		

5. **SOUNDING OUT SMOOTHLY** Have students sound out the word in one smooth breath, then read the word.

♥♥   sneered   picked   clucked

6. **MULTISYLLABIC WORDS** Have students silently figure out each word and read it aloud.

| ✎✎ | barnyard | lesson | impressed |
| ✈✈ | expect | bragging | however |

★7. **TRICKY WORDS** See Teacher's Guide for how to introduce "Once," "pretty," and "head." Next, have students silently figure out each word and read it aloud.

✿   ★ Once   ★ pretty   ★ head   gone

8. **DAILY STORY READING**

29

◆◆ **SENTENCE SUGGESTIONS**

● **each** – **Point to each student.** *Each* of you can read well.

● **such** – It was *such* a good story we wanted to read it again.

☆ **while** – *While* I read, please follow the words with your finger.

☆ **white** – **Point to something white.** This is a *white* [shirt].

✎ **vain** – Someone who is too proud of his or her looks is *vain*.

✈ **snooty** – Someone who is *snooty* thinks he or she is better than everyone else.

✈ **witty** – Someone who is *witty* is funny.

✿ **Once** – The story began, "*Once* upon a time."

✿ **pretty** – Someone or something that is nice to look at is . . . *pretty*.

✿ **head** – Touch your *head*.

Sentence Suggestions: If a sentence is included, use it *after* decoding the individual word. The sentences may be used to build oral language patterns and vocabulary. Use of sentences also emphasizes that words have meaning.

1 INTRODUCING THE UNIT AND THE TITLE PAGE

Identifying—Title

Remind students that the whole book is called *Fact or Fiction*.
Tell students this unit is called "The Chicken and the Egg."

Making Connections, Classifying

In Unit 36 we read stories that were either fact or fiction.
The stories about frog and fish rain were . . . (fact).
We also read a story about Mother Goose and a
frog that flew. That story was . . . (fiction).

This unit is called "The Chicken and the Egg."
What do you think we'll learn about?
When we read this unit, think about whether
the story is fact or fiction.

Priming Background Knowledge

Ask students what they already know about chickens.

2 INTRODUCING VOCABULARY

Vocabulary—Hen, Rooster, Vain, Lesson; Classifying

Hen

Put your finger under the first picture.
A *hen* is a grown-up girl chicken.
Do you think a hen is a mammal or a bird?

Rooster

Put your finger under the next picture.
A *rooster* is a grown-up boy chicken.
Do you think a rooster is a mammal or a bird?
What does a rooster say?

Vain

Someone who is too proud of his or her looks is . . . (vain).
Someone who is *vain* might spend a lot of time looking in a mirror, thinking
"I'm so handsome" or "I'm so pretty."

Lesson

A *lesson* is something that you learn.

The Chicken and the Egg

By Marilyn Sprick
Illustrated by Nicole in den Bosch

UNIT 37 STORIES

Vocabulary Words

hen	rooster	vain	lesson
A hen is a grown-up girl chicken.	A rooster is a grown-up boy chicken.	Someone who is too proud of his or her looks is vain.	A lesson is something that you learn.

22   23

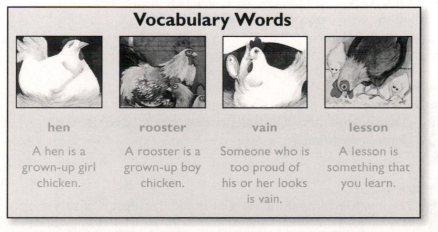

Vocabulary Words

hen	rooster	vain	lesson
A hen is a grown-up girl chicken.	A rooster is a grown-up boy chicken.	Someone who is too proud of his or her looks is vain.	A lesson is something that you learn.

Defining Vocabulary—Hen, Rooster, Vain, Lesson

SOLO STORY READING INSTRUCTIONS

Students read from their own storybooks.

COMPREHENSION BUILDING: DISCUSSION QUESTIONS AND TEACHER THINK ALOUDS

- Ask questions and discuss text on the *second* reading when indicated in the storybook in light gray text.
- Encourage students to answer questions with complete sentences when appropriate.
- If students have difficulty with a comprehension question, think aloud with them or reread the portion of the story that answers the question. Then, ask the question again.

PROCEDURES

Applying Vocabulary—Vain; Classifying

1. Introduction

- Have students read the title of the story. Say something like:

  Your new story is called "The Vain Hen."

  What kind of hen is this story going to be about? (A vain hen)

  What do you already know about one of the characters?

  (She is a hen who thinks she is really pretty.)

  Do you think this story is going to be fact or fiction?

2. First Reading

- Have students individually whisper read the story, using their fingers to track text.
- After students complete the first reading and before the second reading, have students practice a few paragraphs. Encourage expressive reading. Acknowledge student efforts and demonstrate as needed.

3. Second Reading

- Mix group and individual turns, independent of your voice. Have students work toward an accuracy goal of 0–2 errors. Quietly keep track of errors made by all students in each group.
- After reading the story, practice any difficult words.
- If the group has not reached the accuracy goal, have the group reread the story, mixing group and individual turns.

4. Repeated Readings

a. Partner Reading

During students' daily independent work, have them do Partner Reading.

b. Homework 1

Have students read the story at home. (A reprint of this story is available on a blackline master in *Read Well* Homework.)

Note: Questions focus students on important story elements and provide prompts for story discussions. Answers provide guidance, not verbatim responses.

The Vain Hen

CHAPTER 1
Chuckella

Once upon a time, there was a pretty white hen named Chuckella. Chuckella had gotten many prizes because she was so pretty. This had gone to her head. Each morning she would sing, "I'm so pretty. I'm pretty, and witty, and wise . . . "

The other chickens, however, were not impressed! They would sing, "Cluck, cluck, yuck. She's pretty, and snooty, and vain!"

Who is this story's main character?**1** How does Chuckella describe herself?**2** How do the other chickens describe Chuckella?**3**

24

1 Identifying—Who (The main character is a hen named Chuckella.)

2 Describing (She says she is pretty, witty, and wise.)

3 Describing (They say she is pretty, snooty, and vain.)

Each day, Farmer Brown's wife, Jane, would come to the hen house and gather eggs from the hens. Then she would take the eggs to the market to sell.

What would Jane do each day? **1** Where would Jane take the hens' eggs to sell? **2**

25

❶ **Identifying—Action** (She would gather eggs from the hens.)

❷ **Identifying—Where** (She would take their eggs to the market.)

STORY 1, SOLO

When Chuckella began laying eggs, Jane said, "Chuckella is so pretty. We shouldn't sell her eggs. We should let Chuckella hatch her eggs." Chuckella clucked to the rest of the hens, "I'm so pretty. I will have such pretty chicks!"

Why did Jane think they should let Chuckella hatch her eggs instead of selling them? **1** How do you think the other hens might feel about Chuckella getting to hatch her eggs? **2**

26

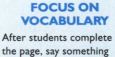

FOCUS ON VOCABULARY

After students complete the page, say something like:

Who is the *vain* hen in this story? (Chuckella)

Now we've learned that Chuckella is going to get special treatment. Oh dear. I wonder if that will make her even more snooty and vain. What do you think?

❶ Explaining (She thought Chuckella was pretty. She thought they should let Chuckella's eggs hatch because the chicks would be pretty too.)

❷ Inferring

SOUND PAGE

Use work pages from the workbook.

UNIT **37** SKILL WORK ACTIVITY 1a
SOUND PAGE: For use after Story 1

Name _____ ▲

Ch ch

✓ chill

Ch Ch Ch Ch Ch

ch ch ch ch ch ch

ch ch ch ch ch ch

71

PROCEDURES

For each step, demonstrate and guide practice as needed.

1. Handwriting—Basic Instructions

- Have students identify the letter combination <u>ch</u> as in "chicken."
- Have students trace and write the capital letter combination <u>Ch</u>—leaving a finger space between each combination. Repeat with the small letter combination <u>ch</u> on the last rows.
- In each row have students circle their best letter combination.

2. Drawing Pictures That Use /ch/—Basic Instructions

- Have students fill the box with things that use /ch/. Students can write the letters <u>ch</u>, draw pictures of things that use /ch/, cut out and paste on pictures of things that use /ch/, or cut out and paste on words that use /ch/.

Note: Neat work helps students take pride in their efforts. Periodically, comment on students' progress and best efforts.

STORY COMPREHENSION

Use work pages from the workbook.

Monitoring Comprehension
Locating Information

Identifying—Who

Writing
Describing
Conventions—Period

Identifying—Where

Writing
Explaining
Conventions—Period

Writing
Classifying
Conventions—Period

CHECKOUT OPPORTUNITY

Listen to your students read individually while others work.

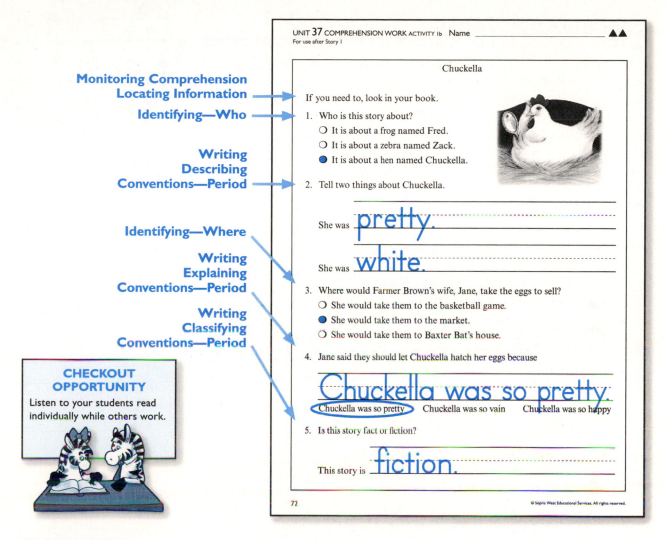

UNIT **37** COMPREHENSION WORK ACTIVITY 1b **Name** _____ ▲▲
For use after Story 1

Chuckella

If you need to, look in your book.

1. Who is this story about?
   ○ It is about a frog named Fred.
   ○ It is about a zebra named Zack.
   ● It is about a hen named Chuckella.

2. Tell two things about Chuckella.

   She was _pretty._

   She was _white._

3. Where would Farmer Brown's wife, Jane, take the eggs to sell?
   ○ She would take them to the basketball game.
   ● She would take them to the market.
   ○ She would take them to Baxter Bat's house.

4. Jane said they should let Chuckella hatch her eggs because

   Chuckella was so pretty.

   (Chuckella was so pretty)   Chuckella was so vain   Chuckella was so happy

5. Is this story fact or fiction?

   This story is _fiction._

72   © Sopris West Educational Services. All rights reserved.

PROCEDURES

For each step, demonstrate and guide practice as needed.

- (Demonstrate) Have students orally respond to items while you demonstrate how to complete the page.
- (Guide) Have students orally respond to the items, but do not demonstrate how to complete the page.
- (Independent With Support) Have students silently read over the items and ask any questions they may have.

1. **Multiple Choice—Basic Instructions** (Items 1, 3)
   Have students fill in the bubble for the correct answer.

2. **Sentence Completion—Basic Instructions** (Items 2, 5)
   - Have students read the direction or question and brainstorm possible responses.
   - Have students complete the sentence and end with a period.

3. **Multiple Choice, Sentence Completion—Basic Instructions** (Item 4)
   - Have students select and circle the words that correctly complete the sentence.
   - Have them write the answer in the blank and end the sentence with a period.

SOLO STORY READING INSTRUCTIONS
Students read from their own storybooks.

COMPREHENSION BUILDING:
DISCUSSION QUESTIONS AND TEACHER THINK ALOUDS
- Ask questions and discuss text on the *second* reading when indicated in the storybook in light gray text.
- Encourage students to answer questions with complete sentences when appropriate.
- If students have difficulty with a comprehension question, think aloud with them or reread the portion of the story that answers the question. Then, ask the question again.

PROCEDURES

1. Introduction
After students read the chapter title and answer the questions, say something like:

Do you think this story is fact or fiction?
What makes you think it's fiction? (The chickens talk.)

2. First Reading
- Have students individually whisper read the story, using their fingers to track text.
- After students complete the first reading and before the second reading, have students practice a paragraph. First demonstrate expressive reading for students, then give individual turns. Acknowledge student efforts.

3. Second Reading
- Mix group and individual turns, independent of your voice.
  Have students work toward an accuracy goal of 0–2 errors.
  Quietly keep track of errors made by all students in each group.
- After reading the story, practice any difficult words.
- If the group has not reached the accuracy goal, have the group reread the story, mixing group and individual turns.

4. Repeated Readings

a. Timed Readings

- Once the accuracy goal has been achieved, have individual students read the page while the other children track the text with their fingers and whisper read.
  Time individuals for 30 seconds and encourage each student to work for a personal best.
- Count the number of words read correctly in 30 seconds (words read minus errors). Multiply by two to determine words correct per minute. Record student scores.

b. Partner Reading

During students' daily independent work, have them do Partner Reading.

c. Homework 2

Have students read the story at home. (A reprint of this story is available on a blackline master in *Read Well Homework*.)

CHAPTER 2

Chuckella Needs a Lesson

Who is the main character? [1] A lesson is something that is learned. What do you think Chuckella needs to learn? [2]

The hen house was buzzing. The other hens were very upset when they found out that Chuckella would get to hatch her eggs. "Cluck, cluck, cluck. Did you hear? Chuckella gets to hatch her eggs!"

Chuckella sneered, "What do you expect? I win prizes because I am such a pretty hen. My chicks will be pretty too!"

The hens got together and said, "Cluck, cluck, cluck. We need to teach Chuckella a lesson."

The next day, while Chuckella was out in the barnyard, the hens picked two chicken eggs from Chuckella's nest. Into the nest they set one very small white egg and one big black egg.

When Chuckella came back, she didn't even see that the eggs were different. She just got on her nest and started bragging, "I'm so pretty."

Why were the other hens upset? [3] What did the other hens think Chuckella needed? [4] What did the hens do? [5]

27

❶ **Summarizing, Identifying—Main Character** (The main character is Chuckella.)

❷ **Inferring** (She needs to learn to be nicer—not so vain.)

❸ **Explaining, Inferring** (They were upset because Chuckella got to hatch her eggs. They were upset because Chuckella bragged.)

❹ **Identifying—What** (She needed to be taught a lesson.)

❺ **Identifying—Action** (They took the two chicken eggs out of Chuckella's nest and put a small white egg and a big black egg in the nest.)

STORY 2, SOLO

What did Chuckella do about the different eggs in her nest?**1** What do you think might happen next?**2**

28

1 **Explaining, Identifying—Action** (Chuckella just sat on her eggs. She didn't notice that the eggs were different.)

2 **Predicting**

24

STORY COMPREHENSION

Use work pages from the workbook..

Monitoring Comprehension
Locating Information

Writing
Describing
Conventions—Period

Writing
Identifying—Goal
Conventions—Period

Identifying—What

Identifying—What

Writing
Predicting
Conventions—Period

CHECKOUT OPPORTUNITY
Listen to your students read individually while others work.

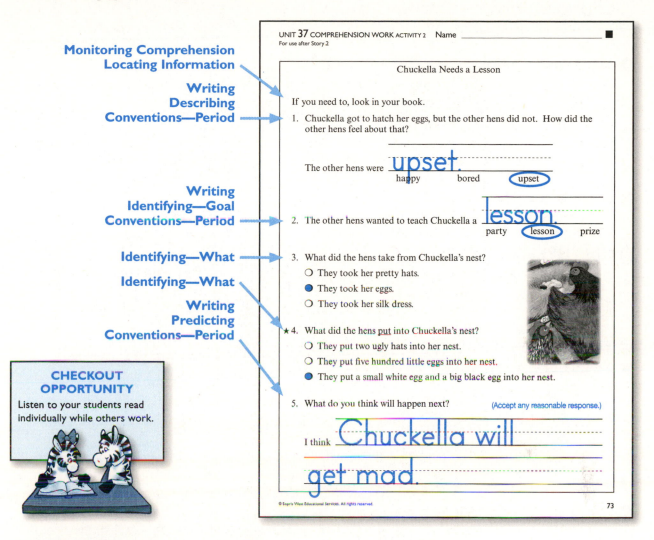

UNIT **37** COMPREHENSION WORK ACTIVITY 2   Name _____ ■
For use after Story 2

Chuckella Needs a Lesson

If you need to, look in your book.

1. Chuckella got to hatch her eggs, but the other hens did not. How did the other hens feel about that?

   The other hens were **upset.**

   happy   bored   (upset)

2. The other hens wanted to teach Chuckella a **lesson.**

   party   (lesson)   prize

3. What did the hens take from Chuckella's nest?
   ○ They took her pretty hats.
   ● They took her eggs.
   ○ They took her silk dress.

★ 4. What did the hens put into Chuckella's nest?
   ○ They put two ugly hats into her nest.
   ○ They put five hundred little eggs into her nest.
   ● They put a small white egg and a big black egg into her nest.

5. What do you think will happen next?   (Accept any reasonable response.)

   I think **Chuckella will get mad.**

73

PROCEDURES

For each step, demonstrate and guide practice as needed.
If students are unsure of the answers, have them look in their books.

1. **Multiple Choice, Sentence Completion—Basic Instructions** (Items 1, 2)
   • Have students select and circle the word that correctly completes the sentence.
   • Have them write the answer in the blank and end the sentence with a period.

2. **Multiple Choice—Basic Instructions** (Items 3, 4)
   Have students fill in the bubble for the correct answer. Periodically, think aloud with students. Discuss the multiple choice options. As appropriate, ask questions like: "Does the first answer make sense?" "Is that what the book said?" "Is the answer completely correct?"

   Note: In Item 4, students are required to read the Tricky Word "put," which has not yet been introduced. Teach the word if necessary.

3. **Sentence Completion—Basic Instructions** (Item 5)
   • Have students read the question and brainstorm possible responses.
   • Have students complete the sentence and end it with a period.

①　SOUND REVIEW

②　SOUNDING OUT SMOOTHLY

Provide repeated practice. Mix group and individual turns, independent of your voice.

③　ACCURACY AND FLUENCY BUILDING

Repeat practice on each column, building accuracy first and then fluency.

Note: For the Airplane Column, remind students that the Bossy E will make the letter i in each word say its name. The Triangle Column provides practice in discriminating between the long and short sounds for a and i. Have students identify what the underlined letter says before they read each word. Prompt them to look for the Bossy E if necessary.

④　SOUNDING OUT SMOOTHLY

Provide repeated practice. Mix group and individual turns, independent of your voice.

⑤　MULTISYLLABIC WORDS

- Have students silently figure out each word, then read it. Use the words in sentences as needed.
- Provide repeated practice. Mix group and individual turns, independent of your voice.

◆◆　⑥　TRICKY WORDS

★ **New Tricky Words: "dinosaur," "does"**

- For the word "dinosaur," have students try to figure the word out themselves. Tell students the correct pronunciation, if needed, then have them read the word "dinosaur" three times.
- Tell students their next new Tricky Word is "does." Have students read the word "does" three times.
- Have students read the row. Repeat, mixing group and individual turns, independent of your voice. Use the words in sentences as needed.

⑦　DAILY STORY READING

Proceed to the Unit 37 Storybook. See Daily Lesson Planning for pacing suggestions.

⑧　COMPREHENSION AND SKILL WORK ACTIVITY 3 AND/OR ACTIVITY 4

See pages 32, 33, and/or 37, 38.

Note: The light scripting in *Read Well* will help you visualize instruction as you prepare for a lesson. Scripting provides an instructional guide and is not intended to be memorized or read to students.

◆◆　For ELLs and children with language delays, provide repeated and extended practice with the language patterns.

UNIT **37** DECODING PRACTICE 2
(For use with Stories 3 and 4)

1. SOUND REVIEW Use Sound Cards for Units 1–37 or Sound Review on Decoding Practice 4.

2. SOUNDING OUT SMOOTHLY For each word, have students say any underlined part, then read the word.

■ h<u>a</u>tch   sw<u>itch</u>ing   sp<u>ee</u>ch   sp<u>ee</u>chless

ACKNOWLEDGE ACCOMPLISHMENTS
Students love concrete acknowledgment of their accomplishments. As students are reading a row or column, say: You got one right, two right, three right!

3. ACCURACY/FLUENCY BUILDING For each column, have students say any underlined part, then read each word. Next, have students read the column.

♥	✏	✈	▲
how			l<u>i</u>ck
now	v<u>ai</u>n	wh<u>i</u>le	l<u>i</u>ke
about	r<u>ai</u>n	crocod<u>i</u>le	l<u>a</u>ck
snout	tr<u>ai</u>n	l<u>i</u>ke	l<u>a</u>ke

4. SOUNDING OUT SMOOTHLY Have students sound out the word in one smooth breath, then read the word.

♥♥ snake   Zeb   goose   peeked

5. MULTISYLLABIC WORDS Have students say each word part, then read the whole word.

✏✏ ribbit   fossil   robin   indeed   seven

✈✈ ev•¢ry•one = everyone   cack•led = cackled

◆◆ SENTENCE SUGGESTIONS

✏✏ ribbit – The frog said, "*Ribbit* . . . ribbit."

✏✏ fossil – An old, old dinosaur bone would be a *fossil*.

✿ does – What *does* a [rooster] say?

★6. TRICKY WORDS See the Teacher's Guide for how to introduce "dinosaur" and "does." Next, have students silently figure out each word, then read it aloud.

✿ ★dinosaur   ★does   laugh   pretty   once

7. DAILY STORY READING
30

Sentence Suggestions: Use the appropriate suggested sentence *after* decoding each individual word.

SOLO STORY READING INSTRUCTIONS

Students read from their own storybooks.

COMPREHENSION BUILDING:
DISCUSSION QUESTIONS AND TEACHER THINK ALOUDS

- Ask questions and discuss text on the *second* reading when indicated in the storybook in light gray text.
- Encourage students to answer questions with complete sentences when appropriate.
- If students have difficulty with a comprehension question, think aloud with them or reread the portion of the story that answers the question. Then, ask the question again.

PROCEDURES

1. Summarizing

After students read the chapter title, say something like:

Who is the main character? (Chuckella)

What is her problem? (She is vain.)

The chickens are trying to teach Chuckella not to be so . . . vain.

What trick did they pull in the last chapter? (They took two of Chuckella's eggs and put two other eggs in her nest.)

Do you think tricking Chuckella will teach her to be nicer and not so vain?

2. First Reading

- Have students individually whisper read the story, using their fingers to track text.
- After students complete the first reading and before the second reading, have students practice a paragraph. Encourage expressive reading, then give individual turns. Acknowledge student efforts and demonstrate if needed.

3. Second Reading

- Mix group and individual turns, independent of your voice.
  Have students work toward an accuracy goal of 0–2 errors.
  Quietly keep track of errors made by all students in each group.
- After reading the story, practice any difficult words.
- If the group has not reached the accuracy goal, have the group reread the story, mixing group and individual turns.

4. Repeated Readings

a. Partner Reading

During students' daily independent work, have them do Partner Reading.

b. Homework 2

Have students read the story at home. (A reprint of this story is available on a blackline master in *Read Well* Homework.)

CHAPTER 3

Switching Eggs

Every time Chuckella left her nest, the hens would switch more eggs. Out came a chicken egg, in went a crocodile egg. Out came a chicken egg, in went a small snake egg.

Even Zeb the Rooster got into the act. Out came a chicken egg, in went a big, hard dinosaur egg.

"Where did you get that fossil?" the hens asked Zeb.

"Farmer Brown found it, but then he forgot about it," said Zeb.

Name two kinds of eggs the hens put in Chuckella's nest.**I** What did Zeb the Rooster put in the nest?**2**

29

❶ **Identifying—What** (The hens put a crocodile egg and a snake egg in the nest.)
❷ **Identifying—What** (Zeb put a dinosaur egg in the nest. It was a fossil.)

At last, Chuckella had seven eggs in her nest. Not one was a chicken egg, but Chuckella couldn't tell!

How many eggs did Chuckella end up with in her nest? ▌

30

❶ **Identifying** (She had seven eggs in her nest.)

Chuckella looked at the eggs and asked, "Now what?"

The hens clucked, "Now you sit there until all your eggs hatch!"

Chuckella was not happy. She asked, "Who will see me while I sit on my nest all day?"

The hens cackled, "We will, dear. We will!"

What did the hens tell Chuckella she needed to do?**1** Why didn't Chuckella want to sit on her nest?**2**

31

FOCUS ON VOCABULARY

After students complete the page, say something like:

What on this page tells us that Chuckella was *vain*? (She wanted others to see her.)

Do you think tricking Chuckella will help her learn to be nicer?

❶ Identifying—What (They said she needed to sit on her nest until the eggs hatched.)

❷ Explaining (She was afraid no one would see her if she was sitting on her nest.)

STORY COMPREHENSION

Use work pages from the workbook.

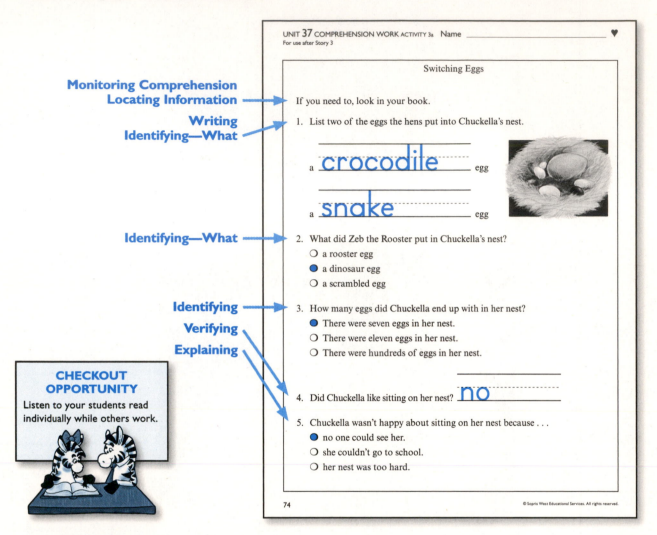

Monitoring Comprehension
Locating Information
Writing
Identifying—What

Identifying—What

Identifying
Verifying
Explaining

CHECKOUT OPPORTUNITY
Listen to your students read individually while others work.

UNIT **37** COMPREHENSION WORK ACTIVITY 3a Name _____

For use after Story 3

Switching Eggs

If you need to, look in your book.

1. List two of the eggs the hens put into Chuckella's nest.

a __crocodile__ egg

a __snake__ egg

2. What did Zeb the Rooster put in Chuckella's nest?
   ○ a rooster egg
   ● a dinosaur egg
   ○ a scrambled egg

3. How many eggs did Chuckella end up with in her nest?
   ● There were seven eggs in her nest.
   ○ There were eleven eggs in her nest.
   ○ There were hundreds of eggs in her nest.

4. Did Chuckella like sitting on her nest? __no__

5. Chuckella wasn't happy about sitting on her nest because . . .
   ● no one could see her.
   ○ she couldn't go to school.
   ○ her nest was too hard.

74   © Sopris West Educational Services. All rights reserved.

PROCEDURES

For each step, demonstrate and guide practice as needed.

1. List—Basic Instructions (Item 1)
   • Have students read the direction and brainstorm possible responses.
   • Have students write the answers in the blanks.

2. Multiple Choice—Basic Instructions (Items 2, 3, 5)
Have students fill in the bubble for the correct answer.

3. Question Response—Basic Instructions (Item 4)
Have students read the question and answer "yes" or "no" in the blank.

RHYMING PATTERNS

Use work pages from the workbook.

UNIT **37** SKILL WORK ACTIVITY 3b
RHYMING PATTERNS: For use after Story 3

Name _____

(n) (f) (sh) (x̶)	(d) (x̶) (h) (f)	(cl) (x̶) (br) (t)
ine	ive	own
nine	dive	clown
fine	hive	brown
shine	five	town

(x̶) (ch) (r) (v)	(sh) (gr) (x̶) (t)	(m) (x̶) (h) (bl)
ain	ape	ouse
chain	shape	mouse
rain	grape	house
vain	tape	blouse

75

CHECKOUT OPPORTUNITY

Listen to your students read individually while others work.

PROCEDURES

Demonstrate and guide practice as needed.

Rhyming Patterns—Basic Instructions

For each box, have students:

- Read the rhyming pattern.
- Circle the three sounds above the rhyming pattern that go with it to make real words.
- Cross out the sound that does not make a real word with the rhyming pattern.
- Write the three rhyming words on the lines provided.

Note: For students who struggle or who lack the English language base to know which are real words, you may wish to identify the three sounds they should circle in each box. Students can then write the pattern words on their own.

SOLO STORY READING INSTRUCTIONS

Students read from their own storybooks.

COMPREHENSION BUILDING: DISCUSSION QUESTIONS AND TEACHER THINK ALOUDS

- Ask questions and discuss text on the *second* reading when indicated in the storybook in light gray text.
- Encourage students to answer questions with complete sentences when appropriate.
- If students have difficulty with a comprehension question, think aloud with them or reread the portion of the story that answers the question. Then, ask the question again.

PROCEDURES

1. Summarizing

Have student read the chapter title. Then ask:

Who is the main character in this story? (Chuckella is the main character.)

What is Chuckella's problem? (She is vain. She brags. She thinks she is better than the other hens.)

What are the other hens trying to do? (They are trying to teach Chuckella a lesson.)

What lesson are the hens and the rooster trying to teach Chuckella? (They are trying to teach Chuckella not to be so snooty and vain.)

2. First Reading

- Have students individually whisper read the story, using their fingers to track text.
- After students complete the first reading and before the second reading, have students practice a paragraph. First demonstrate expressive reading for students, then give individual turns. Acknowledge student efforts.

3. Second Reading

- Mix group and individual turns, independent of your voice. Have students work toward an accuracy goal of 0–2 errors. Quietly keep track of errors made by all students in each group.
- After reading the story, practice any difficult words.
- If the group has not reached the accuracy goal, have the group reread the story, mixing group and individual turns.

4. Repeated Readings

a. Timed Readings

- Once the accuracy goal has been achieved, have individual students read the page while the other children track the text with their fingers and whisper read.

Time individuals for 30 seconds. Determine words correct per minute. Record student scores.

b. Partner Reading

During students' daily independent work, have them do Partner Reading.

c. Homework 2

Have students read the story at home. (A reprint of this story is available on a blackline master in *Read Well Homework*.)

CHAPTER 4
Until the Dinosaur Hatches

When her eggs started to crack, Chuckella sneered, "Now everyone will see how pretty my chicks are!"

Just then Chuckella peeked at the chick that was hatching. It had a long green snout! Chuckella was speechless. The other hens clucked, "Pretty chick indeed!"

When Chuckella's eggs were done hatching, there was a crocodile-like *chick*, a snake-like *chick*, a robin-like *chick*, and a goose-like *chick*. There was even a little green *chick* that said "Ribbit, ribbit." There were no pretty little chicks. The hens laughed and laughed.

Chuckella said, "So what! There's one egg left. It will be my pretty little chick."

Zeb said, "Chuckella, that egg isn't going to hatch. It's a dinosaur egg."

Chuckella wouldn't listen. To this day, she is still sitting on that big, hard dinosaur egg.

What hatched from Chuckella's eggs?**1** What did Chuckella say?**2** One egg didn't hatch. Why not?**3** What is Chuckella doing now?**4** Do you think Chuckella has learned her lesson?**5**

32

❶ Identifying—What (A baby crocodile, snake, robin, goose, and frog hatched.)

❷ Identifying—What (She said, "So what!" Then she said the last chick would be pretty.)

❸ Explaining (It was a fossil—the dinosaur egg. It wasn't going to hatch.)

❹ Explaining (She is still sitting on that egg—waiting for it to hatch into a pretty chick!)

❺ Evaluating

33

36

STORY MAP

Use work pages from the workbook.

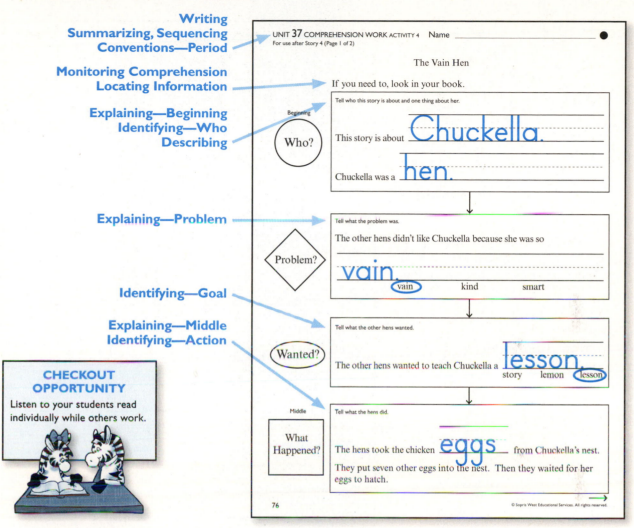

Writing
Summarizing, Sequencing
Conventions—Period

Monitoring Comprehension
Locating Information

Explaining—Beginning
Identifying—Who
Describing

Explaining—Problem

Identifying—Goal

Explaining—Middle
Identifying—Action

CHECKOUT OPPORTUNITY
Listen to your students read individually while others work.

UNIT 37 COMPREHENSION WORK ACTIVITY 4 Name _____
For use after Story 4 (Page 1 of 2)

The Vain Hen

If you need to, look in your book.

Beginning

Who?
Tell who this story is about and one thing about her.
This story is about __Chuckella.__
Chuckella was a __hen.__

Problem?
Tell what the problem was.
The other hens didn't like Chuckella because she was so
__vain.__
(vain)   kind   smart

Wanted?
Tell what the other hens wanted.
The other hens wanted to teach Chuckella a __lesson.__
story   lemon   (lesson)

Middle

What Happened?
Tell what the hens did.
The hens took the chicken __eggs__ from Chuckella's nest.
They put seven other eggs into the nest. Then they waited for her eggs to hatch.

76

PROCEDURES

For each step, demonstrate and guide practice as needed.

Story Map—Basic Instructions

- Using a blank or overhead copy of the story map, help students identify the basic story elements—who the story is about, what the problem was, what the characters wanted, what happened in the story, and what happened at the end.
- Have students fill in the blanks to create a story map of "The Vain Hen."
- Remind students that a story map helps them retell or summarize the important parts of a story.

★ *Note:* If you choose, have students complete the challenge item and write a different ending for the story.

Explaining—End

Inferring

**Writing,
Composing—End
Conventions—Beginning Capital,
Period**

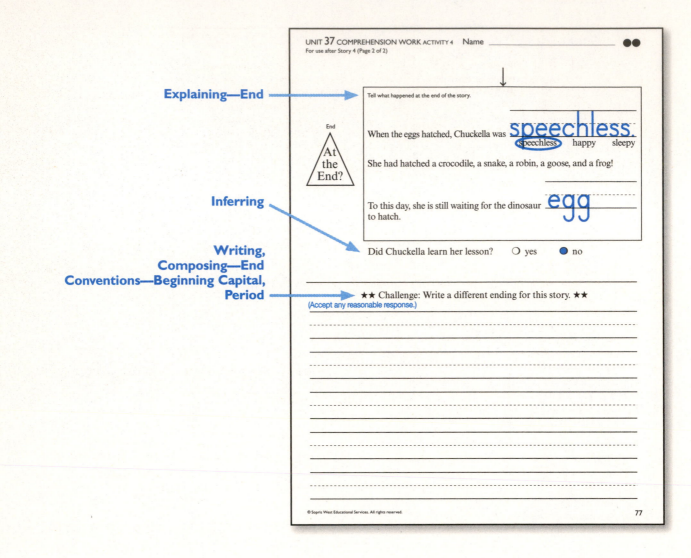

UNIT 37 COMPREHENSION WORK ACTIVITY 4   Name _____   ●●
For use after Story 4 (Page 2 of 2)

Tell what happened at the end of the story.

End

△ At the End?

When the eggs hatched, Chuckella was **speechless.**

(speechless)   happy   sleepy

She had hatched a crocodile, a snake, a robin, a goose, and a frog!

To this day, she is still waiting for the dinosaur **egg** to hatch.

Did Chuckella learn her lesson?   ○ yes   ● no

★★ Challenge: Write a different ending for this story. ★★
(Accept any reasonable response.)

77

Research Snapshot

STORY MAPPING

Numerous studies with older students and low-achieving students have demonstrated that story grammars and story mapping can be used to promote students' understanding of narrative stories (Beck & McKeown, 1981; Carnine & Kinder, 1985; Idol & Croll, 1987; Nolte & Singer, 1985). Baumann and Bergeron (1993) studied the effects of story mapping with first graders. "Results of this study affirm the findings of prior research on story mapping, namely, that teaching students about story parts enables them to recognize and recall important elements in narrative selections (p. 431)." This study validates the usefulness of story mapping with young children.

In *Read Well 1*, students began working with story maps at Unit 21. Practice was repeated and extended in Units 22, 23, 24, 25, 26, 28, 29, 30, 31, 32, 34, 35, 36, 37, and a final map is found in Unit 38. See *Read Well Plus* for use of story mapping to facilitate story comparisons.

1 SOUND REVIEW

◆◆ **2 SOUNDING OUT SMOOTHLY**

Provide repeated practice. Mix group and individual turns, independent of your voice.

3 ACCURACY AND FLUENCY BUILDING

Repeat practice on each column, building accuracy first and then fluency.

4 SOUNDING OUT SMOOTHLY

Provide repeated practice. Mix group and individual turns, independent of your voice.

5 MULTISYLLABIC WORDS

• Have students say each word part, then read the whole word.
Use the words in sentences as needed.
• Provide repeated practice. Mix group and individual turns, independent of your voice.

6 TRICKY WORDS

Have students read the row. Repeat, mixing group and individual turns, independent of your voice. Use the words in sentences as needed.

7 DAILY STORY READING

Proceed to the Unit 37 Storybook. See Daily Lesson Planning for pacing suggestions.

8 COMPREHENSION AND SKILL WORK ACTIVITY 5 AND/OR ACTIVITY 6

See pages 45 and/or 50, 51.

◆◆ For ELLs and children with language delays, provide repeated and extended practice with the language patterns.

UNIT **37** DECODING PRACTICE 3
(For use with Stories 5 and 6)

ACCURACY, THEN RATE
(Reminder)
Practice the words in each row or column until students can read the words with accuracy and confidence. Then work on gradually building speed. Say something like: Let's see if you can read the Heart, Pencil, and Airplane Columns about this fast . . .

1. SOUND REVIEW Use Sound Cards for Units 1–37 or Sound Review on Decoding Practice 4.

2. SOUNDING OUT SMOOTHLY For each word, have students say any underlined part, then read the word.

❀	ea<u>ch</u>	whi<u>ch</u>	bun<u>ch</u>
❀❀	<u>ch</u>icks	<u>ch</u>eep	<u>ch</u>ickens

3. ACCURACY/FLUENCY BUILDING For each column, have students say any underlined part, then read each word. Next, have students read the column.

♥	✎	✈
forming	t<u>i</u>me	m<u>a</u>te
peeking	l<u>i</u>fe	<u>a</u>te
dripping	w<u>i</u>de	<u>ou</u>t
laying	ins<u>i</u>de	sh<u>ou</u>t
beginning		sh<u>or</u>t

4. SOUNDING OUT SMOOTHLY Have students sound out the word in one smooth breath, then read the word.

●	safe	specks	fluffs	fifteen

5. MULTISYLLABIC WORDS Have students say each word part, then read the whole word.

■	them • selves = themselves	de • vel • op • ing = developing

◆◆ **SENTENCE SUGGESTIONS**
❀ which – *Which* story did you like the best?

6. TRICKY WORDS Have students silently figure out each word and then read it aloud.

▲	Once	head	does	their

7. DAILY STORY READING

31

Sentence Suggestions: Use the appropriate suggested sentence *after* decoding each individual word.

SOLO STORY READING INSTRUCTIONS

Students read from their own storybooks.

COMPREHENSION BUILDING:
DISCUSSION QUESTIONS AND TEACHER THINK ALOUDS

- Ask questions and discuss text on the *first* reading when indicated in the storybook in light gray text.
- Encourage students to answer questions with complete sentences when appropriate.
- If students have difficulty with a comprehension question, think aloud with them or reread the portion of the story that answers the question. Then, ask the question again.

PROCEDURES

1. Introducing the Story

The last story was about a vain chicken named Chuckella.

Was the story fact or fiction? (Fiction)

The next passage is called "A Chicken's Life." What is the passage about? (A chicken's life)

As we read the story, think about how a chicken develops. We learned that a frog began with an egg. A tadpole grew inside the egg and hatched. Then, it grew legs and became a frog. This process is called a life cycle. As we read about a chicken's life, think about the stages it goes through in its life.

This passage is not fiction; it's . . . fact.

2. First Reading

- Mix group and individual turns, independent of your voice.
  Have students work toward an accuracy goal of 0–2 errors.
  Quietly keep track of errors made by all students in each group.
- After reading the story, practice any difficult words.
- If the group has not reached the accuracy goal, have the group reread the story, mixing group and individual turns.

3. Second Reading

Have students individually whisper read the story, using their fingers to track text.

Follow the special discussion questions for the second reading.

4. Repeated Readings

a. Partner Reading

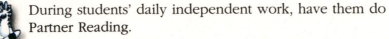

During students' daily independent work, have them do Partner Reading.

b. Homework 3

Have students read the story at home. (A reprint of this story is available on a blackline master in *Read Well* Homework.)

STORY 5, SOLO

A Chicken's Life

CHAPTER I

Life in the Egg

What do you already know about chickens? **I**

Every chicken begins life the same way—as an egg. This is what happens. A hen and a rooster mate. Then the hen lays between seven and fifteen eggs. She lays one egg each day in her nest. Then the hen sits on the eggs until they hatch. She sits and sits for twenty-one days. The mother hen must sit on her eggs to keep them from getting cold. She leaves the nest just to get food and water.

How many eggs does a hen lay? **2** What does the hen do when she leaves her eggs? **3**

Once the hen lays the eggs, little chicks begin to form inside each of the eggs. At the start, the chicks seem to be little red specks in the eggs. In time, the specks get bigger.

Where do the little chicks start to form? **4**

34

FOCUS ON COMPREHENSION
Second Reading
For the second reading, have students read the first paragraph silently.
Prior to reading the paragraph, say something like: Read the first paragraph. It ends at the picture. It tells about the first stage of a chicken's life. Find out what happens after a hen and a rooster mate.
When students finish reading the first paragraph, ask:
After the hen and rooster mate, what does the hen do? (Lay eggs)
An egg is the beginning of a chicken's life cycle.

Read the next paragraph to find out what happens first in the egg.
When students finish reading the paragraph, ask:
What happens first in the egg? (The little chick is just a little red speck.)

❶ **Priming Background Knowledge**

❷ **Identifying—Fact** (A hen lays seven to fifteen eggs.)

❸ **Identifying—Action, Explaining** (She gets food and water.)

❹ **Identifying—Where** (The little chicks begin to form inside the eggs.)

After two days, the heads of the chicks are forming. After seven days, the beginnings of their legs and wings develop—all inside the egg. Soon their beaks develop. All this time, the mother hen sits on her nest, getting off just for food and water.

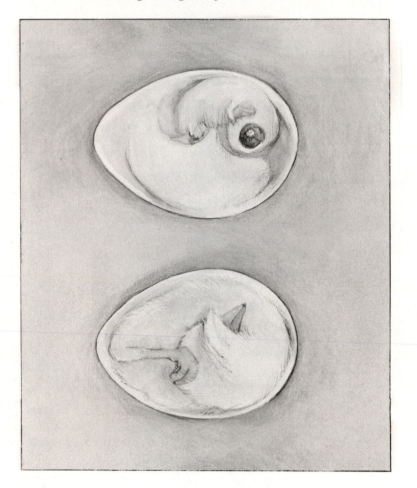

What does the mother hen do while her chicks are developing in their eggs? |

35

❶ **Identifying—Action** (She sits on the eggs in her nest.)

REPORT WRITING

Use work pages from the workbook.

Monitoring Comprehension
Locating Information

Writing
Identifying—Topic
Conventions—Period

Writing
Identifying—Fact

Writing
Identifying—Fact

Writing
Identifying—Fact

Illustrating—Action

UNIT **37** COMPREHENSION WORK ACTIVITY 5   Name _____
For use after Story 5

My Report on a Chicken's Life, Part 1

If you need to, look in your book.

In this chapter, I learned many facts about **chickens.**

1. I learned that chickens lay between **seven** and **fifteen** eggs.

2. Once a hen lays her eggs, she **sits** on them until they hatch.

3. Little chicks begin to form **inside** each egg.
outside   (inside)

Mother hens sit on their nests.

78
© Sopris West Educational Services. All rights reserved.

CHECKOUT OPPORTUNITY
Listen to your students read individually while others work.

PROCEDURES

Explain to your students that they will be writing a report about what they've learned.

1. **Sentence Completion—Basic Instructions** (Topic Sentence, Items 1–2)

   Have students read, complete each sentence, and end each sentence with a period as appropriate.

2. **Multiple Choice, Sentence Completion—Basic Instructions** (Item 3)
   • Have students select and circle the correct word.
   • Have them write the answer in the blank and place a period at the end.

3. **Sentence Illustration—Specific Instructions**

   Have students read the sentence and then complete the illustration.

SOLO STORY READING INSTRUCTIONS

Students read from their own storybooks.

COMPREHENSION BUILDING: DISCUSSION QUESTIONS AND TEACHER THINK ALOUDS

- Ask questions and discuss text on the *second* reading when indicated in the storybook in light gray text.
- Encourage students to answer questions with complete sentences when appropriate.
- If students have difficulty with a comprehension question, think aloud with them or reread the portion of the story that answers the question. Then, ask the question again.

PROCEDURES

1. First Reading

- Mix group and individual turns, independent of your voice. Have students work toward an accuracy goal of 0–2 errors. Quietly keep track of errors made by all students in each group.
- After reading the story, practice any difficult words.
- If the group has not reached the accuracy goal, have the group reread the story, mixing group and individual turns.

2. Second Reading

Have students individually whisper read the story, using their fingers to track text.

Follow the special discussion questions for the second reading.

3. Repeated Readings

a. Timed Readings

- Once the accuracy goal has been achieved, have individual students read the page while the other children track the text with their fingers and whisper read.

Time individuals for 30 seconds and encourage each student to work for a personal best.

- Count the number of words read correctly in 30 seconds (words read minus errors). Multiply by two to determine words correct per minute. Record student scores.

b. Partner Reading

During students' daily independent work, have them do Partner Reading.

c. Homework 4

Have students read the story at home. (A reprint of this story is available on a blackline master in *Read Well* Homework.)

STORY 6, SOLO

CHAPTER 2

Life in the Barnyard

After twenty-one days in the eggs, the little chicks run out of food. They become so big that they need to get out of their shells. They peck, peck, peck.

How many days until little chicks hatch?**1**

All chicks have a tooth called an egg tooth. The egg tooth helps them crack their shells. They peck thousands of times to crack their shells.

What does a little chick have that helps it crack open its shell?**2**

When they get out, the chicks are dripping wet and not very pretty. After a short time, they fluff up. Soon they can eat. They can get around by themselves, and say, "Cheep, cheep, cheep." Before long, the little chicks become roosters and hens.

What does a newly hatched chick look like?**3**What will a little chick become in time?**4**

Then, just as their mothers and fathers did, the hens and roosters will mate. The hens will lay eggs. Soon another bunch of chicks will develop, hatch, and become hens and roosters. It's all part of life in the barnyard.

36

> **FOCUS ON COMPREHENSION**
> **Second Reading**
> Have students read the page silently. Say something like: You're going to read the passage again to yourself. Read to find out what happens to the chicken after twenty-one days.
> After students read, say something like:
> At the beginning of the chicken's life cycle, there was an . . . egg. In the egg there was a little red speck. For the next twenty-one . . . days, the little red speck developed into a chick. What happened next? (The chick pecked out of the shell. After the chick got out of the shell, it grew up and became a hen or a rooster.)

❶ **Identifying** (Little chicks hatch after twenty-one days.)

❷ **Identifying—What** (A chick has an egg tooth.)

❸ **Describing** (A new chick is dripping wet and not very pretty.)

❹ **Identifying—What** (The chick will become a hen or a rooster.)

37

COMPREHENSION BUILDING: FACT SUMMARY

The text of this fact summary leads students through the life cycle of a chicken. Sentence starters help students answer in complete sentences.

FACT SUMMARY

A Chicken's Life

Let's review four of the facts we learned about chickens.[1]

_____

Fact one: Where does every chicken begin life?

Start your answer with "Every chicken begins life in . . ."[2]

_____

Fact two: How many days does it take for the chick to hatch out of the egg?

Start your answer with "It takes . . ."[3]

_____

Fact three: What does the chick have that helps it crack open the shell?

Start your answer with "The chick has an . . ."[4]

_____

Fact four: After a short time, what does the chick become?

Start your answer with "The chick becomes a . . ."[5]

38

---

❶ **Summarizing, Building Knowledge**

❷ **Identifying—Fact** (Every chicken begins life in an egg.)

❸ **Identifying—Fact** (It takes twenty-one days for a chick to hatch.)

❹ **Identifying—Fact** (The chick has an egg tooth that it uses to crack open the egg.)

❺ **Identifying—Fact** (The chick becomes a hen or a rooster.)

REPORT WRITING

Use work pages from the workbook.

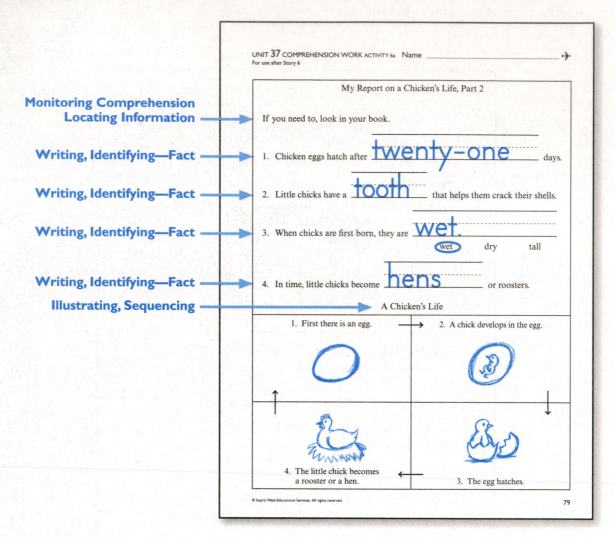

Monitoring Comprehension
Locating Information

Writing, Identifying—Fact

Writing, Identifying—Fact

Writing, Identifying—Fact

Writing, Identifying—Fact

Illustrating, Sequencing

UNIT 37 COMPREHENSION WORK ACTIVITY 6a   Name _____
For use after Story 6

My Report on a Chicken's Life, Part 2

If you need to, look in your book.

1. Chicken eggs hatch after **twenty-one** ____ days.

2. Little chicks have a **tooth** ____ that helps them crack their shells.

3. When chicks are first born, they are **wet.**
   (wet)   dry   tall

4. In time, little chicks become **hens** ____ or roosters.

A Chicken's Life

1. First there is an egg.   2. A chick develops in the egg.

4. The little chick becomes a rooster or a hen.   3. The egg hatches.

© Sopris West Educational Services. All rights reserved.   79

PROCEDURES

Explain to your students that they will be writing a report about what they've learned.

1. **Sentence Completion—Basic Instructions** (Items 1, 2, 4)
   Have students read, complete each sentence, and end each sentence with a period as appropriate.

2. **Multiple Choice, Sentence Completion—Basic Instructions** (Item 3)
   • Have students select and circle the correct word.
   • Have them write the answer in the blank and place a period at the end.

3. **Sentence Illustration—Specific Instructions**
   Have students read each sentence and then complete each illustration.

STORY COMPREHENSION

Use work pages from the workbook.

CHECKOUT OPPORTUNITY

Listen to your students read individually while others work.

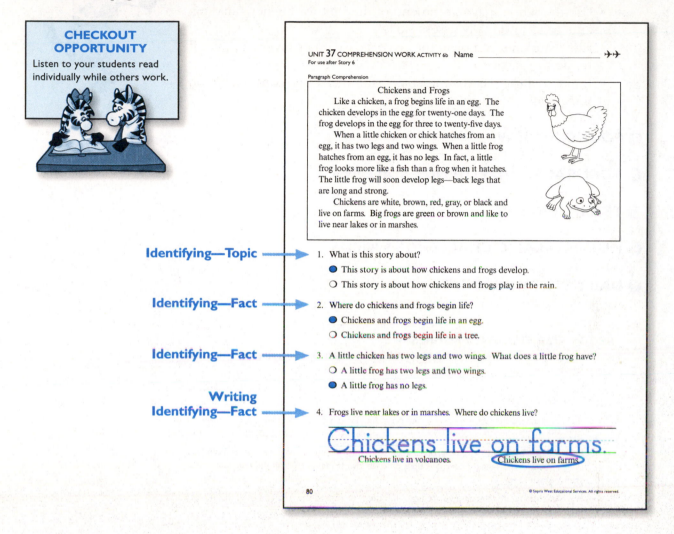

UNIT **37** COMPREHENSION WORK ACTIVITY 6b Name _____

For use after Story 6

Paragraph Comprehension

Chickens and Frogs

Like a chicken, a frog begins life in an egg. The chicken develops in the egg for twenty-one days. The frog develops in the egg for three to twenty-five days.

When a little chicken or chick hatches from an egg, it has two legs and two wings. When a little frog hatches from an egg, it has no legs. In fact, a little frog looks more like a fish than a frog when it hatches. The little frog will soon develop legs—back legs that are long and strong.

Chickens are white, brown, red, gray, or black and live on farms. Big frogs are green or brown and like to live near lakes or in marshes.

Identifying—Topic

1. What is this story about?
   - ● This story is about how chickens and frogs develop.
   - ○ This story is about how chickens and frogs play in the rain.

Identifying—Fact

2. Where do chickens and frogs begin life?
   - ● Chickens and frogs begin life in an egg.
   - ○ Chickens and frogs begin life in a tree.

Identifying—Fact

3. A little chicken has two legs and two wings. What does a little frog have?
   - ○ A little frog has two legs and two wings.
   - ● A little frog has no legs.

**Writing
Identifying—Fact**

4. Frogs live near lakes or in marshes. Where do chickens live?

Chickens live on farms.

Chickens live in volcanoes.   Chickens live on farms

80   © Sopris West Educational Services. All rights reserved.

PROCEDURES

For each step, demonstrate and guide practice as needed.

1. Paragraph Comprehension—Basic Instructions

- Have students read the paragraph to themselves.
- Have students fill in the bubble for the correct answer.
- Have students write a complete sentence that starts with a capital letter and ends with a period.

Note: There are multiple uses for Decoding Practice 4.

- Have students practice a few rows and/or columns each day.
- Use the whole page at the end of the unit for fluency building and/or to informally assess skills.
- Have students complete the page as a partner review or take it home to practice.
- Build spelling dictation lessons using the sounds and words on this page.

❶ SOUND REVIEW

❷ ACCURACY AND FLUENCY BUILDING

❸ TRICKY WORDS

❹ MULTISYLLABIC CHALLENGE WORDS

❺ DAILY STORY READING

See Daily Lesson Planning for story suggestions.

RECOGNIZE STUDENT PROGRESS

As students are reaching the end of *Read Well*, you may wish to remind students of just how much they've learned.

1. Have students reread the first unit they read in *Read Well*, only this time let them also read the teacher text!

2. Pick an old Solo Story from early in the program. Time individual students for one minute on the story. They will be amazed to see how many times they can read a passage in one minute!

3. Let students pick a favorite unit. Have each student practice reading the stories from this unit, including the teacher text. Set up a time for the students to read the unit stories to younger students.

4. Have each student select a favorite unit. Tell them to reread the unit and then make a list of interesting facts they learned.

UNIT **37** DECODING PRACTICE 4
(See Daily Lesson Planning for story suggestions.)

✈

1. **SOUND REVIEW** Set pace. Have students read the sounds in each row.

●	ch	ea	X	ou	S	wh	u	7
♥	z	oo	g	qu	Ch	ow	d	14
■	m	V	ar	h	t	e	C	21

2. **ACCURACY/FLUENCY BUILDING** For each column, have students say any underlined part, then read each word. Next, have students read the column.

✈	✈✈	✿	✿✿	✿✿✿
each	rain	ch<u>a</u>p	b<u>i</u>t	T<u>i</u>m
teach	train	ch<u>i</u>p	f<u>i</u>ne	t<u>i</u>me
reach	brain	ch<u>o</u>p	M<u>i</u>ke	t<u>a</u>me
preach	chain	ch<u>ee</u>p	h<u>i</u>d	t<u>ea</u>m
bleach	vain	ch<u>u</u>mp	sl<u>i</u>de	T<u>o</u>m

3. **TRICKY WORDS** Have students silently figure out each word and then read it aloud.

★★	Pretty	laugh	very	water	many
☆★	Their	once	because	don't	again

4. **MULTISYLLABIC CHALLENGE WORDS** Have students say each word part, then read the whole word.

chim · pan · zee = chimpanzee	fic tion
chat · ter · box = chatterbox	frac tion
scratch · y = scratchy	ad di tion

5. **DAILY STORY READING**

32

End of the Unit

In this section, you will find:

Making Decisions

As you near the end of the unit, you will need to make decisions. Should you administer the Oral Reading Fluency Assessment or should you teach Extra Practice lessons?

Unit 37 Oral Reading Fluency Assessment

The Unit 37 Oral Reading Fluency Assessment is located on page 56 and can also be found in the *Assessment Manual*.

Certificate of Achievement

Celebrate your children's accomplishments.

Extra Practice

Lessons and blackline masters for added decoding practice and independent work are provided for students who need extended practice opportunities.

Making Decisions

ASSESSMENT READINESS

Assess when students are able to easily complete decoding tasks from the beginning of a lesson.

- If you aren't sure whether students are ready for the assessment, give the assessment. Do Extra Practice lessons if needed.
- If students are not ready for the assessment, proceed to Extra Practice lessons. Administer the assessment as soon as students are ready.

GENERAL ASSESSMENT GUIDELINES

- Assess all students.
- Assess each child individually.
- Score student responses on the Student Assessment Record, adhering to the scoring criteria in the *Assessment Manual*. Use a stopwatch to time how long it takes the student to read the oral fluency passage.
- Follow the general instructions at the bottom of each assessment. Record a Strong Pass, a Pass, a Weak Pass, or a No Pass.

ACCELERATION

- If students read with 100% accuracy and exceed the fluency goal, consider shortening units.
- If an individual student reads with greater fluency than others in his or her group, consider regrouping.

> **ASSESSING UNPRACTICED READING**
>
> Do not have children practice the assessments. The goal of reading instruction is to provide children with the skills to read independently. Repeated readings are an excellent tool for building fluency; however, the end-of-the-unit assessment is designed to assess how well students transfer their skills to unrehearsed passages.

INTERVENTION OPTIONS—INDIVIDUALS
(WEAK PASS, NO PASS)

1. Add informal practice throughout the day.
2. Add practice with repeated readings on Solo Stories.
3. Find ways to provide a double dose of *Read Well* instruction.
   - Have the student work in his or her group *and* a lower group.
   - Have an instructional assistant, older student, or parent volunteer preview or review lessons.
   - Have an instructional assistant provide instruction with Extra Practice lessons.
4. Consider placement in a lower group. If one child's fluency scores are significantly lower than the other children in the group, success will be impossible without additional and intensive practice.

INTERVENTION OPTIONS—GROUP (WEAK PASS, NO PASS)

1. Extend the unit with Extra Practice lessons.
2. Consider a Jell-Well Review before moving forward. (See the *Assessment Manual*.)

CERTIFICATE OF ACHIEVEMENT

When students pass the assessment, celebrate with the Certificate of Achievement. Then, set a personal goal. (See *Getting Started*.)

TRICKY WORD WARM-UP

many	laugh	pretty	head	their

ORAL READING FLUENCY PASSAGE

Chuck the Frog

★ Once upon a time, there was a little green frog named Chuck.   12

He was such a funny frog that he could make everyone laugh   24

out loud.   26

Each day, Chuck would tell the other frogs a funny story.   37

They would laugh so hard that they would fall down. At last,   49

two of the frogs said, "Chuck, we really like you. But we can't   62

take this laughing anymore."   66

Chuck was speechless. He stopped being funny.   73

Soon, the other frogs were very sad. They said, "Chuck, we   84

need a funny story."   88

Chuck said, "I have just the story for you."   97

ORAL READING FLUENCY	Start timing at the ★ Mark errors. Make a single slash in the text (/) at 60 seconds. Have student complete passage. If the student completes the passage in less than 60 seconds, have the student go back to the ★ and continue reading. Make a double slash (//) in the text at 60 seconds.
WCPM	Determine words correct per minute by subtracting errors from words read in 60 seconds.
STRONG PASS	The student scores no more than 2 errors on the first pass through the passage and reads a minimum of 98 or more words correct per minute. Proceed to Unit 38.
PASS	The student scores no more than 2 errors on the first pass through the passage and reads 78 to 97 words correct per minute. Proceed to Unit 38.
WEAK PASS	The student scores no more than 2 errors on the first pass through the passage and reads 59 to 77 words correct per minute. Proceed to Unit 38 with added fluency practice, or provide Extra Practice lessons in Unit 37, and/or provide a Jell-Well Review.
NO PASS	The student scores 3 or more errors on the first pass through the passage and/or reads 58 or fewer words correct per minute. Provide Extra Practice lessons and retest, and/or provide a Jell-Well Review.

Certificate of Achievement

This certifies that

_____,

on this _____ day of _____, _____,

has successfully completed

Read Well Unit 37

Sounds Mastered: s, e, ee, m, a, d, th, n, t, w, i, Th, h, c, r, ea, sh, k, -ck, oo, ar, wh, ĕ, -y (as in "fly"), l, o, b, all, g, f, u, -er, oo (as in "book"), y, a (schwa), p, ay, v, qu, j, x, or, z, a_e, -y (as in "baby"), i_e, ou, ow, ch, ai

Known Words: By Unit 36, you had learned and practiced 1,360 words.

New Words Mastered in Unit 37: addition, crocodile, develop, developing, dinosaur, does, fathers, head, heads, lesson, mothers, once, pretty, themselves, barnyard, beaks, begin, beginning, beginnings, begins, between, bit, bleach, bragging, brain, bunch, buzzing, cackled, chain, chap, chatterbox, cheep, chick, chicken, chickens, chicken's, chicks, chimpanzee, chip, chop, Chuckella, Chuckella's, chuckle, chump, cluck, clucked, each, fluff, fluffs, form, forming, fossil, fraction, gather, gotten, hatch, hatches, hatching, impressed, indeed, inside, laying, lays, life, mate, Mike, morning, named, peeked, peeking, preach, prizes, reach, ribbit, robin, rooster, roosters, safe, scratchy, she's, side, slide, snake, sneered, snooty, snout, specks, speech, speechless, such, switch, switching, teach, time, times, train, vain, which, while, white, wide, wife, wise, witty, Zeb

You can now read 1,465 words—plus many other words made up of the sounds and patterns you've learned.

Note: Personal and Team Goal Setting forms can be copied from Units 16 and 17, or from *Getting Started*.

❶ SOUNDS

❷ WORD DICTATION

such, just, hard, loud

The first word is "such." We're going to count the sounds in "such."
Tell me the first sound. **Hold up one finger.** (/sss/)
Repeat with /uuu/ and /ch/.
How many sounds are in "such"? (Three)

Tell me the first sound. (/sss/) Write it.
Tell me the next sound. (/uuu/) Write it.
Tell me the next sound. (/ch/) Write it with the letter c and the letter h.
Do Smooth Blending. (/sssuuuch/) Read the word. (such)

Repeat with "just," "hard," and "loud." Tell students the /ar/ in "hard" is spelled with the letter <u>a</u> and the letter <u>r</u>. Tell students the /ou/ in "loud" is spelled with the letter <u>o</u> and the letter <u>u</u>.

> **CAUTION**
> Your children may not need Extra Practice. If in doubt, assess students and include Extra Practice only if needed.

> **DICTATION**
> • Demonstrate and guide practice as needed.
> • Have students check and correct.

❸ SENTENCE COMPLETION

Chuck was *a green frog.*

• Have students read the beginning of the sentence with you.
• Dictate the last three words, "a green frog." Remind students to leave a finger space between each word.
• Have students trace the dotted words and complete the sentence with a period.
• Have students read the sentence.

❹ ACCURACY AND FLUENCY BUILDING

❺ TRICKY WORDS

❻ DAILY STORY READING

1. First Reading

Have students choral read the Fluency Passage.

2. Second Reading

• Provide individual turns on sentences. Quietly keep track of errors.
• After reading, practice any difficult words.

3. Repeated Readings
a. Timed Readings

• Have individual students read the passage while other students track the text with their fingers and whisper read. Time individuals for 30 seconds. Encourage students to work for a personal best.

• For each student, determine words correct per minute. Record students' scores.

b. Partner Reading—
Checkout Opportunity

While students are partner reading, listen to individuals read the passage.

1. SOUNDS Have students say each sound.

ch	ou	Z	h	-y	er	X	qu
J	u	v	Ch	or	p	sh	ow

2. WORD DICTATION Have students count the sounds in each word, identify and write each sound, and then read the words: "such," "just," "hard," and "loud."

- - - - - - - - - -   - - - - - - - - - -   - - - - - - - - - -   - - - - - - - - - -

1 _____   2 _____   3 _____   4 _____

3. SENTENCE COMPLETION Have students read the beginning of the sentence. Dictate "a green frog." Have students trace the words and complete the sentence with a period.

Chuck was _____

4. ACCURACY/FLUENCY BUILDING In each column, have students say any underlined part, then read each word. Next, have students read the column.

♥	♥♥	♥♥♥
h<u>a</u>tch	<u>t</u>ime	upon
<u>ea</u>ch	t<u>a</u>ke	everyone
sp<u>ee</u>ch	m<u>a</u>ke	anymore
<u>i</u>tch	M<u>i</u>ke	speechless
s<u>u</u>ch	l<u>i</u>ke	however

5. TRICKY WORDS For each word, have students silently figure out the word, then read it aloud.

laugh	many	two	head	does

6. DAILY STORY READING

Name_____

FLUENCY PASSAGE

Chuck the Frog

The little green frog named Chuck was sad. He had	10
stopped being funny and he no longer made everyone laugh.	20
Chuck just sat on a rock looking upset. The other frogs were	32
sad. When Chuck would tell a funny story, they would fall	43
down. They didn't want Chuck to make them fall all the	54
time. What could they do?	59

My personal best is _____ words correct per minute.

My goal is to read with 0–2 errors. This is what I did:

Have students read the sentences. Time individual students for 30 seconds; mark errors. To determine words correct per minute (wcpm), count words read in 30 seconds, subtract errors, multiply times two, and record on the chart. If the student completes the passage in less than 30 seconds, have him or her return to the top and continue reading. (Repeated readings may be completed with older students, assistants, or parents.)

Reading	1st	2nd	3rd	4th
Errors				
Words/ 30 seconds				
wcpm				

60

Take-Home Game

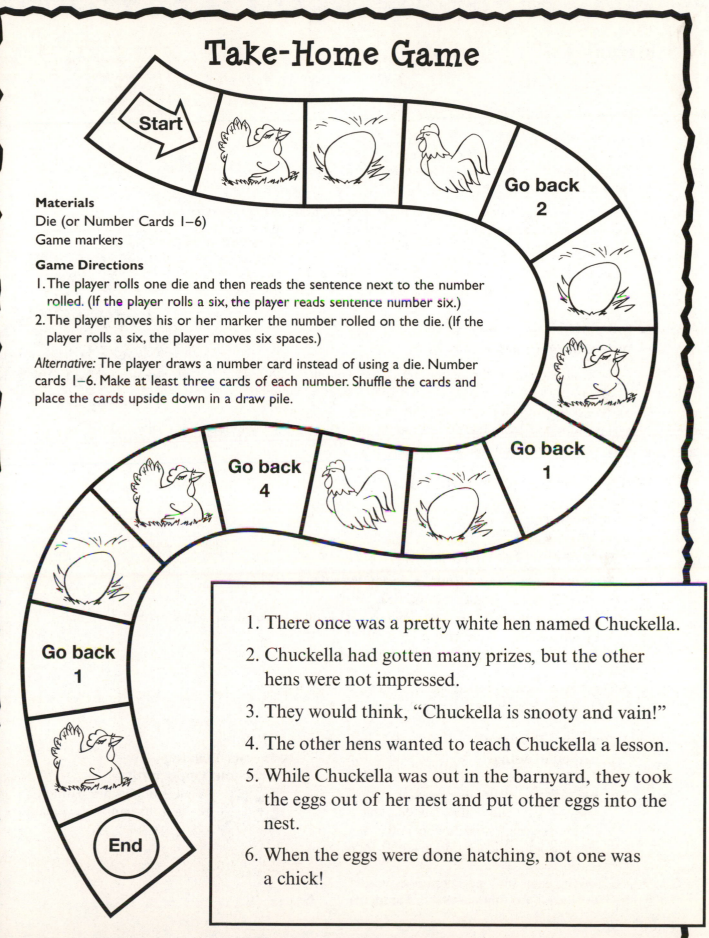

Start

Go back 2

Go back 1

Go back 4

Go back 1

End

Materials
Die (or Number Cards 1–6)
Game markers

Game Directions
1. The player rolls one die and then reads the sentence next to the number rolled. (If the player rolls a six, the player reads sentence number six.)
2. The player moves his or her marker the number rolled on the die. (If the player rolls a six, the player moves six spaces.)

Alternative: The player draws a number card instead of using a die. Number cards 1–6. Make at least three cards of each number. Shuffle the cards and place the cards upside down in a draw pile.

1. There once was a pretty white hen named Chuckella.

2. Chuckella had gotten many prizes, but the other hens were not impressed.

3. They would think, "Chuckella is snooty and vain!"

4. The other hens wanted to teach Chuckella a lesson.

5. While Chuckella was out in the barnyard, they took the eggs out of her nest and put other eggs into the nest.

6. When the eggs were done hatching, not one was a chick!

① **SOUNDS**

② **WORD DICTATION**

each, out, for, frog

The first word is "each." We're going to count the sounds in "each."
Tell me the first sound. **Hold up one finger.** (/eaeaea/)
Tell me the next sound. **Hold up two fingers.** (/ch/)
How many sounds are in "each"? (Two)

Tell me the first sound. (/eaeaea/) Write it with the letter <u>e</u> and the letter <u>a</u>.
Tell me the next sound. (/ch/) Write it with the letter <u>c</u> and the letter <u>h</u>.
Do Smooth Blending. (/eaeaeach/) Read the word. (each)

Repeat with "out," "for," and "frog." Tell students that the /ou/ in "out" is spelled with the letter <u>o</u> and the letter <u>u</u>.

HAVE STUDENTS CHECK AND CORRECT.

③ **SENTENCE COMPLETION**

We could *jump down*.

- Have students read the beginning of the sentence with you.
- Dictate the last two words "jump down." Remind students to leave a finger space between each word.
- Have students trace the dotted words and complete the sentence with a period.
- Have students read the sentence.

④ **ACCURACY AND FLUENCY BUILDING**

⑤ **TRICKY WORDS**

⑥ **DAILY STORY READING**

1. First and Second Readings, Fluency Passage A
- Have students choral read the text.
- Provide individual turns on sentences. Quietly keep track of errors made by all students in the group.
- After reading, practice any difficult words.

2. First and Second Readings, Fluency Passage B
Repeat step one with Fluency Passage B.

3. Repeated Readings
  a. Timed Readings

  - Have individual students read either passage A or B while other students track the text with their fingers and whisper read. Time individuals for 30 seconds.
  - For each student, determine words correct per minute. Record students' scores.

  b. Partner Reading—
  Checkout Opportunity

  While students are partner reading, listen to individuals read a passage.

1. **SOUNDS** Have students say each sound.

z	ow	Ch	ay	or	wh	b	U
ch	-y	d	ar	P	ou	c	ea

2. **WORD DICTATION** Have students count the sounds in each word, identify and write each sound, and then read the words: "each," "out," "for," and "frog."

1 _____   2 _____   3 _____   4 _____

3. **SENTENCE COMPLETION** Have students read the beginning of the sentence. Dictate "jump down." Have students trace the words and complete the sentence with a period.

We could _____

4. **ACCURACY/FLUENCY BUILDING** In each column, have students say any underlined part, then read each word. Next, have students read the column.

♥	♥♥	♥♥♥
ch<u>u</u>ck	being	funny
ch<u>i</u>ck	laughing	story
ch<u>e</u>ck	laughed	really
ch<u>o</u>mp	named	pretty
ch<u>a</u>mp	stopped	very

5. **TRICKY WORDS** For each word, have students silently figure out the word, then read it aloud.

Once	pretty	their	other	don't

6. **DAILY STORY READING**

Name_____

FLUENCY PASSAGE A

Clever Frog	
One clever frog said, "We can help Chuck be happy."	10
That smart frog had a plan. That afternoon the frogs took	21
Chuck to the big hall. They all sat down on mats on the	34
floor.	35

FLUENCY PASSAGE B

Funny Frog	
The frogs had Chuck go to the front. They said, "Tell	11
us a funny story. Make us laugh!" Soon, everyone was	21
falling on the mats. The frogs all said, "Let's do this every	33
week." Chuck was happy.	37

My personal best is _____ words correct per minute.
My goal is to read with 0–2 errors. This is what I did:

Have students read the sentences. Time individual students for 30 seconds on one passage; mark errors. To determine words correct per minute (wcpm), count words read in 30 seconds, subtract errors, multiply times two, and record on the chart. If the student completes the passage in less than 30 seconds, have him or her return to the top and continue reading. (Repeated readings may be completed with older students, assistants, or parents.)

Reading	1st	2nd	3rd	4th
Errors				
Words/ 30 seconds				
wcpm				

❶ STORYBOOK DECODING REVIEW

For each row, mix group and individual turns, independent of your voice.

❷ WORD DICTATION

Have students count the sounds in each word with their fingers, identify and write each sound, and then read the word. Use the words in sentences as needed.

day, But, last, need

The first word is "day." We're going to count the sounds in "day."
Tell me the first sound. **Hold up one finger.** (/d/)
Tell me the next sound. **Hold up two fingers.** (/ay/)
How many sounds are in "day"? (Two)

Tell me the first sound. (/d/) Write it.
Tell me the next sound. (/ay/) Write it with the letter <u>a</u> and the letter <u>y</u>.
Do Smooth Blending. (/day/) Read the word. (day)

Repeat with "But," "last," and "need."

> **CAUTION**
>
> Your children may not need Extra Practice. If in doubt, assess students and include Extra Practice only if needed.

> **HAVE STUDENTS CHECK AND CORRECT.**

❸ DAILY STORY READING

1. First Reading

Have students choral read the Fluency Passage.

2. Second Reading

- Provide individual turns on sentences. Quietly keep track of errors made by all students in the group.
- After reading, practice any difficult words.

3. Repeated Readings

a. Timed Readings

- Have individual students read the passage while other students track the text with their fingers and whisper read. Time individuals for 30 seconds. Encourage students to work for a personal best.
- For each student, count the number of words read correctly in 30 seconds (words read minus errors). Multiply by two to determine words correct per minute. Record students' scores.

b. Partner Reading—Checkout Opportunity

While students are partner reading, listen to individuals read the passage. Work on accuracy or fluency as needed.

Name_____

FLUENCY PASSAGE

Chicken Feed

A little chick named Nick was looking for food in the   11
barnyard. He looked and looked near a tree. Then it started   22
to rain. Nick could see a seed he wanted to eat, but it was all   37
wet. Nick wanted to eat the seed but it was so wet he could   51
not get it. So Nick ate the seeds the farmer left out for him.   65

My personal best is _____ words correct per minute.
My goal is to read with 0–2 errors. This is what I did:

Have students read the sentences. Time individual students for 30 seconds; mark errors. To determine words correct per minute (wcpm), count words read in 30 seconds, subtract errors, multiply times two, and record on the chart. If the student completes the passage in less than 30 seconds, have him or her return to the top and continue reading. (Repeated readings may be completed with older students, assistants, or parents.)

Reading	1st	2nd	3rd	4th
Errors				
Words/ 30 seconds				
wcpm				

① DECODING PRACTICE 4 REVIEW

For each row, mix group and individual turns, independent of your voice.

② WORD DICTATION

Have students count the sounds in each word with their fingers, identify and write each sound, and then read the word. Use the words in sentences as needed.

this, Soon, sad, tell

The first word is "this." We're going to count the sounds in "this."
Tell me the first sound. **Hold up one finger.** (/ththth/)
Repeat with /iii/ and /sss/.
How many sounds are in "this"? (Three)

Tell me the first sound. (/ththth/) Write it.
Repeat with /iii/ and /sss/.
Do Smooth Blending. (/thththiiisss/) Read the word. (this)

Repeat with "Soon," "sad," and "tell."

③ DAILY STORY READING

1. First Reading

Have students choral read the Fluency Passage.

2. Second Reading

- Provide individual turns on sentences. Quietly keep track of errors made by all students in the group.
- After reading, practice any difficult words.

3. Repeated Readings
a. Timed Readings

- Have individual students read the passage while other students track the text with their fingers and whisper read. Time individuals for 60 seconds. Encourage students to work for a personal best.
- For each student, count the number of words read correctly in 60 seconds (words read minus errors). Record students' scores.

b. Partner Reading—Checkout Opportunity

While students are partner reading, listen to individuals read the passage. Work on accuracy or fluency as needed.

> **CAUTION**
>
> Your children may not need Extra Practice. If in doubt, assess students and include Extra Practice only if needed.

> **HAVE STUDENTS CHECK AND CORRECT.**

Name_____

FLUENCY PASSAGE

Silly Chickens

Something really funny happened last week. A bunch of   9
chickens from next door got loose. They were running all   19
around my yard. There were little chicks and big chickens.   29
All of them were saying, "Cheep, cheep, cheep." Now, I   39
like chickens, but this was too much.   46

My sister and I started shouting. We were trying to get   57
the chickens in one spot, which was not easy! After a while,   69
we had about forty chickens by the swings. Just then, a   80
white car came down the street. It was the people from next   92
door. They got their chickens back and everyone ended   101
up laughing.   103

My personal best is _____ words correct per minute.

My goal is to read with 0–2 errors. This is what I did:

Have students read the sentences. Time individual students for 60 seconds; mark errors. To determine words correct per minute (wcpm), count words read in 60 seconds, subtract errors, and record on the chart. If the student completes the passage in less than 60 seconds, have him or her return to the top and continue reading. (Repeated readings may be completed with older students, assistants, or parents.)

Reading	1st	2nd	3rd	4th
Errors				
Words/ 60 seconds				
wcpm				